Reading Comprehension:
Teacher Resource
and
Student Activities
Grade 5

BY
DOROTHY NELSON

COPYRIGHT © 2001 Mark Twain Media, Inc.

ISBN 1-58037-152-3

Printing No. CD-1373

Mark Twain Media, Inc., Publishers
Distributed by Carson-Dellosa Publishing Company, Inc.

Table of Contents

Table of Contents

Introduction

Teaching reading <u>is</u> rocket science. Actually, teaching reading is more difficult than rocket science. The teacher, through observation and analysis of various assessments, must "guess" what is happening in the child's mind as he or she reads. Why does she do that? Why did he make that mistake? Why didn't she self-correct? What reading strategies is he using? Why didn't she comprehend what she decoded so well? Why is he such a reluctant reader? And perhaps the biggest question … what do I do next to help that child?

The task of teaching reading becomes a more difficult challenge when a child has *learned to read* in the primary grades and then enters the middle grades. The student is now *reading to learn* in all content areas. The stakes are higher. The student's academic success depends on the control he or she has of the reading process.

Far too many of our students avoid reading and see it only as something expected of them at school. They do not make the important connections between the book and their lives, the book and other reading, or the book and the world. Until our students know how to make those connections, they will never see reading as a meaningful part of their lives.

Reluctant readers will say that they do not remember what they have read. We know it is not that they cannot remember, but that they did not comprehend what they read. Why? Because they did not know how to carry the meaning through the text as they *read the words*. Until our students know how to be strategic readers, they will never be able to use the information they have read to create new understanding and solve problems.

The purpose of this book is to offer scaffolding for reading instruction. First, we need to know our students as readers. This is the teacher's first task and will provide critical information to inform our instruction. We also need to recognize the power of conversation and dialogue about our reading. Next, we need to teach our students the explicit comprehension strategies that good readers use. This is so important in removing the mystery about the reading process. Comprehension is the absence of confusion. It is our greatest challenge to remove that confusion. We need to teach students how to apply these strategies to both fiction and informational texts. Finally, we must teach students to not only generate their own questions, but also how to answer test questions. All teachers are reading teachers. We must ***strategically plan*** to teach explicit reading strategies to support our students' academic success.

Chapter 1: Reading Comprehension and Knowing Your "Kids": *Introduction*

The first and most important step to teaching children to improve their reading is to know each student. We need to know how they see themselves as readers and writers. We need to know what is important to them and what is not important to them. We need to know the people who touch their lives outside the classroom. We need to know what they are proud of and what makes them feel insecure. It is this knowledge that will give us the "hooks" necessary to get the right books into each student's hands.

The following activities can be used as springboards to get to know your students:

Reading Survey (This survey can be given in the following ways.)
- written assignment
- student/teacher conferences
- student/student interviews
- ongoing reflection for student's literacy portfolio

Reading Attitude Survey (This survey can be given in the following ways.)
- written assignment
- student/teacher conferences
- student/student interviews
- ongoing reflection for student's literacy portfolio

Student Self-evaluation of Reading
- At the beginning of the school year, have students complete the self-evaluation independently. Then have students pair and share about their reading habits. Place self-assessment in student's portfolio. Each quarter have students complete a new form and compare their answers to earlier evaluations.

Prompts to Guide Peer Discussion (Use these prompts as part of the following.)
- literature study discussion
- prompts for literature logs
- teacher/student reading conferences
- student/student reading conferences

Reader's and Writer's Notebook
- Use a writer's notebook as an everyday activity in which students THINK ABOUT their reading.

Copies of these activity pages are found in the appendix of this book and can be photocopied for student use.

Name: _____ Date: _____

Chapter 1: Reading Comprehension and Knowing Your "Kids": *Reading Survey*

Directions: Answer the following questions about your reading habits.

1. How many books do you have of your own? _____

2. How many books have you read this month? _____

3. What kinds of books do you like to read? _____

   _____

4. Who is your favorite author? _____

5. What magazines or newspapers do you like to read? _____

   _____

6. How did you learn to read? _____

   _____

7. When you are reading and come to something you don't know, what do you do?

   _____

   _____

8. What makes a good reader? _____

   _____

   _____

9. Do you think you are a good reader? Why or why not? _____

   _____

10. Why do you think reading well is important? _____

    _____

    _____

Name: _____ Date: _____

Chapter 1: Reading Comprehension and Knowing Your "Kids": *Reading Attitude Survey*

Directions: Circle the answer that is most true about you.

How often do you do the following?

A = Often   B = A few times a month   C = Sometimes   D = Never/Almost never

1. Talk to my family or friends about a good book I have read.   A   B   C   D

2. Reread a favorite book.   A   B   C   D

3. Read at home books that are not part of schoolwork.   A   B   C   D

4. Read books by the same author.   A   B   C   D

5. Go to the library to check out a book.   A   B   C   D

How often is each of the following true for you and your reading?

A = Often   B = A few times a month   C = Sometimes   D = Never/Almost never

6. I can understand what I am assigned to read in school.   A   B   C   D

7. I feel proud about how I read.   A   B   C   D

8. I know reading helps me learn about many subjects.   A   B   C   D

9. I enjoy reading aloud in class.   A   B   C   D

10. I like to listen to a book being read aloud.   A   B   C   D

11. I like to read.   A   B   C   D

Name: _____ Date: _____

Chapter 1: Reading Comprehension and Knowing Your "Kids": *Teacher/Student Interview Questions*

About book selection

1. Why do you select a book to read? _____

    _____

2. How do you know the book is one you can read? _____

    _____

Before reading

3. What do you do before you begin to read a story/novel? _____

    _____

4. What do you do before you read a magazine or newspaper article? _____

    _____

5. What do you do before reading a science or social studies textbook? _____

    _____

During reading

6. If you are reading alone and can't figure out a word, what do you do? _____

    _____

7. If you are reading alone and don't know the meaning of a word, what do you do? _____

    _____

8. What do you do if you don't understand paragraphs or whole pages? _____

    _____

After reading

9. What do you think about when you finish your reading? _____

    _____

What else do you want me to know about your reading?

_____

_____

_____

Name: _____ Date: _____

Chapter 1: Reading Comprehension and Knowing Your "Kids": *Student Self-Assessment of Reading*

Directions: Check the box that indicates your level of understanding while reading.

I Can …	I Try	Sometimes	Always
Remember things I already know.			
Make predictions about what will come next.			
Summarize what I read.			
Sound out words I don't know.			
Give people detailed facts about what I have read.			
Make pictures in my mind as I read.			
Figure out what the author means from different parts of my reading.			
Try reading words I don't know.			
Use expression when I read aloud.			
Guess the meaning of a word because it looks like another word I know.			
Break words into syllables.			
Ask questions to myself or to the author as I read.			

Name: _____ Date: _____

Chapter 1: Reading Comprehension and Knowing Your "Kids": *Creating a Reader's/Writer's Notebook*

A wonderful way for students to continue to identify with themselves as readers and writers is to have them keep a reader's/writer's notebook in which they keep running lists of things they read and purposes for which they write.

Below and on the next page are sample pages that can be kept in a reader's/writer's notebook. These pages are found in the appendix of this book and can be photocopied for student use.

What I Read for Myself	What I Read for My Teacher/School

Name: _____ Date: _____

Chapter 1: Reading Comprehension and Knowing Your "Kids": *Creating a Reader's/Writer's Notebook*

What I Write for Myself and to Others	What I Write for My Teacher/School

Chapter 1: Reading Comprehension and Knowing Your "Kids": *Keeping a Reader's Strategy Journal*

We teach students the many <u>skills</u> needed for improving reading. These skills include:

- Finding main idea
- Using context clues for vocabulary
- Analyzing roots, prefixes, and suffixes in vocabulary building
- Teaching analogies
- Making references
- Sequencing
- Using a variety of fix-up strategies
- Many more.

Unfortunately, for many students these skills are not internalized and used independently to apply to new reading. These skills will only become meaningful **strategies** when the student can reflect on and understand how those skills work **when they are actually reading. A skill only becomes a strategy when the student uses it independently in reading.**

We can move our students to use their skills as strategic readers by giving them varied opportunities to reflect on and record what strategies they are using as they read. The type of reflections we want need to be modeled and practiced. When students are first asked to reflect on what they are doing as they read, they will talk about the **content.**

TEACHER

- **Strategically plan to teach the reading strategies that proficient readers use.**

- **Post reading strategies at various places in the room and have students keep a copy in their reader's journal.**

- **Require every student to keep a reader's journal.**

- **Ask students daily to respond in their reader's journal before, during, or after reading literature or informational texts.**

- **Provide students with specific examples of reflective responses. These examples should be authentic responses by the teacher or other students.**

- **Use the response to inform your teaching.**

Chapter 1: Reading Comprehension and Knowing Your "Kids": *Keeping a Reader's Strategy Journal (continued)*

Examples of student responses to strategies used:

Teacher prompt <u>before reading</u>:

"As you read today, think about your 'thinking.' Do you have any questions? Does anything confuse you and need clarifying? Does the story remind you of anything?"

Student response in journal:

"While I was reading, I kept seeing pictures of everything. That is how well the author described everything. I could almost feel how cold it was when they stopped to make camp on the mountain. It reminded me of a story I read before about an airplane that crashed in the mountains and a lot of people froze to death."

Teacher prompt <u>before reading</u>:

"As you read today, ask yourself this question: 'Does this apply to people today?' If so, how?"

Student response in journal:

"I think kids today do have the same problems. There's lots of prejudice. Even in our school there are kids who don't like other kids who are different than they are. Sometimes they don't like them because they are poor, or they are from another country, or they talk differently."

(As students learn to respond specifically to the reading strategies, the teacher can move them to more developed responses with specific reference to the story.)

Chapter 1: Reading Comprehension and Knowing Your "Kids": *Strategies Good Readers Use (Before/During/After Reading)*

- Selects a book appropriate for his or her reading level

- Uses skimming and scanning to review a text

- Uses prior knowledge

- Makes predictions

- Asks questions

- Pauses to reflect, to summarize, to highlight, or take notes

- Uses context clues

- Rereads

- Uses word analysis to figure out unknown words

- Identifies main ideas

- Makes inferences

- Draws conclusions

- Notes cause and effect

- Knows when they do not understand and self-monitors reading

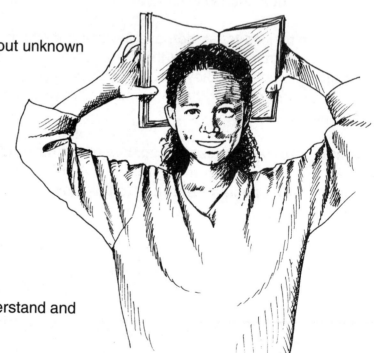

Chapter 2: Reading Comprehension and Talk: *Introduction*

It is important that children learn to talk about books and make connections to their lives, the world, and other books

The following activities can be used as springboards to conversation about books:

Peer Talk: There are seven peer interview opportunities. These interviews can be done in the following ways:

- Students can pair and share their responses before joining a literature study group.
- The interview questions could be used as prompts in their response journals, and students could share these in literature groups.
- Students could answer one of the questions in a quick write. Students could then have an opportunity to share responses with the class in a sharing session.

Think-Pair-Share: Using index cards or small slips of paper, students think about a specific question the teacher has asked about their reading.

- Students write down their thoughts. (Allow only one to two minutes. Hint: Use a timer.)
- Each student turns to a partner and each shares what they wrote. (Allow only one to two minutes.)
- Each student is asked to share the connection made by his or her partner. This part of the activity is most effectively done with the whole class.

Two By Two: This activity can be used to put more explicit instruction into independent reading. In a focus lesson prior to independent reading time, give students a specific purpose for reading.

- Example 1: Teaching Summarizing - "Students, when you finish reading today, be ready to summarize **in one or two sentences** what you read with a partner." Discuss and model what makes a good summary.
- Example 2: Teaching Vocabulary - "Students, as you read today, I want you to write down three of the best words or phrases used by the author. Be ready to share these words and their meanings with a partner."

Hint: After partners share their words, ask each student to share one of his favorite words or phrases. It could be one of his words or one of his partner's. As they share, scribe the words on a flip chart and post the list of words somewhere in the room for future reference. This is a great way to build vocabulary in a meaningful way and to give ownership to the students.

11

Chapter 2: Reading Comprehension and Talk: *Prompts to Guide Peer Discussion*

- What did you like about your book?

- What did you learn?

- How did it make you feel?

- Were there any difficult parts to understand?

- What parts of the story were of special interest to you?

- When you read, did it make you think of other people, places, and/or experiences you'd had?

- What was one of your favorite parts? Why?

- What do you know that you didn't know before you read your book?

- Were there any parts of the book that you would have changed if you had been the author?

- What did you think the author did especially well?

- Would you recommend the book to other classmates? Why or why not?

Name: _____ Date: _____

Chapter 2: Reading Comprehension and Talk: *Peer Talk: The Interview #1*

Directions: After students have read a selection, have them conduct an interview about their reading.

Knowledge:

1. Who are the main characters?

   _____

   _____

   _____

   _____

   _____

2. What do you know about the author?

   _____

   _____

   _____

   _____

   _____

3. What happened in the chapter you read?

   _____

   _____

   _____

   _____

   _____

Name: _____ Date: _____

Chapter 2: Reading Comprehension and Talk: *Peer Talk: The Interview #2*

Directions: After students have read a selection, have them conduct an interview about their reading.

Comprehension:

1. What are two words to describe the main character?

   _____

2. What do you know about the character's personality?

   _____

   _____

   _____

   _____

   _____

3. Retell the story.

   _____

   _____

   _____

   _____

   _____

   _____

   _____

   _____

   _____

Name: _____ Date: _____

Chapter 2: Reading Comprehension and Talk: *Peer Talk: The Interview #3*

Directions: After students have read a selection, have them conduct an interview about their reading.

Application:

1. Create a time line to show what has happened so far in your reading.

2. If you were to write a letter to one of the characters, what would you say?

   _____

   _____

   _____

   _____

   _____

   _____

   _____

   _____

   _____

   _____

3. Draw a picture on your own paper illustrating the most important scene in your reading.

Name: _____ Date: _____

Chapter 2: Reading Comprehension and Talk: *Peer Talk: The Interview #4*

Directions: After students have read a selection, have them conduct an interview about their reading.

Analysis:

1. How would you solve the problem in the story differently if you could?

   _____

   _____

   _____

   _____

2. What do you think is the author's message or main theme?

   _____

   _____

   _____

   _____

3. What other books have you read that have a similar message or theme? How are they different/alike?

   _____

   _____

   _____

   _____

Name: _____ Date: _____

Chapter 2: Reading Comprehension and Talk: *Peer Talk: The Interview #5*

Directions: After students have read a selection, have them conduct an interview about their reading.

Synthesis:

1. What do you predict will happen next?

    _____

    _____

    _____

    _____

2. If a sequel were written to this book, what would happen?

    _____

    _____

    _____

    _____

3. If this book were given an award, what would it receive and why?

    _____

    _____

    _____

    _____

Name: _____ Date: _____

Chapter 2: Reading Comprehension and Talk: *Peer Talk: The Interview #6*

Directions: After students have read a selection, have them conduct an interview about their reading.

Evaluation:

1. Would you recommend the book for other students to read? Why or why not?

   _____

   _____

   _____

   _____

2. Did the characters make the right decisions? Would you have done the same? Why?

   _____

   _____

   _____

   _____

3. Is the theme of the book realistic for students today? Why or why not?

   _____

   _____

   _____

   _____

Name: _____ Date: _____

Chapter 2: Reading Comprehension and Talk: *Peer Talk: The Interview #7*

Directions: After students have read a selection, have them conduct an interview about their reading.

Making Connections:

1. What in the book reminds you of something that happened to you or someone you know?

   _____

   _____

   _____

   _____

2. Did this book remind you of any other book you have read? How are the two books similar?

   _____

   _____

   _____

   _____

3. What was something you learned about life, people, or yourself as you read this book?

   _____

   _____

   _____

   _____

Chapter 2: Reading Comprehension and Talk: *Think-Pair-Share: Activity #1*

Directions: Using index cards or small slips of paper, have students think about and write down their responses to the following question.

THINK ABOUT

When have you experienced something similar to what has happened in the story?

PAIR WITH

Students are to turn to a partner and each will share what they wrote.

SHARE

Students are asked to share the connection made by their partners.

Chapter 2: Reading Comprehension and Talk: *Think-Pair-Share: Activity #2*

Directions: Using index cards or small slips of paper, have students think about and write down their response to the following question:

THINK ABOUT

What other stories or books have you read that have a similar character, plot, problem, or theme?

PAIR WITH

Students are to turn to a partner and each will share what they wrote.

SHARE

Students are asked to share the connection made by their partners.

Chapter 2: Reading Comprehension and Talk: *Think-Pair-Share: Activity #3*

Directions: Using index cards or small slips of paper, have students think about and write down their response to the following question:

THINK ABOUT

What other people or events happening today or that happened in history did this story remind you of?

PAIR WITH

Students are to turn to a partner and each will share what they wrote.

SHARE

Students are asked to share the connection made by their partners.

Chapter 2: Reading Comprehension and Talk: *Two by Two*

Example 1: Teaching Summarizing

(Before reading a chosen book independently during silent sustained reading, students are asked to be prepared to summarize what they have read. After independent reading, students are organized into pairs to do the following activity.)

1. Partner 1 summarizes for partner 2. (Give students a specific time limit of one to two minutes.)

2. Partner 2 (the listener) listens for the main idea or event and retells it to partner 1. Partner 2 then asks his/her partner what he/she likes best about the book.

3. Partner 2 summarizes for partner 1. (Give students a specific time limit of one to two minutes.)

4. Partner 1 (the listener) listens for the main idea or event and retells it to partner 2. Partner 1 asks his/her partner what he/she likes about the book.

    (Teacher may guide students to listen for any reading strategy.)

Example 2: Teaching Vocabulary

(Before reading a chosen book independently during silent sustained reading, students are asked as they read to write down two or three of the author's best words or phrases and think about what each one means. After independent reading, students are organized into pairs to do the following activity.)

1. Partner 1 shares his/her selected words/phrases.

2. Partner 2 (the listener) asks his/her partner the meaning of any word or phrase he/she doesn't know. If the partner is familiar with all of the words, partner 2 should ask why partner 1 thinks the author chose that word or phrase.

3. Partner 2 shares his/her selected words/phrases.

4. Partner 1 (the listener) asks his/her partner the meaning of any word or phrase he/she doesn't know. If the partner is familiar with all of the words, partner 1 should ask why partner 2 thinks the author chose that word or phrase.

5. Each student shares a favorite word or phrase with the whole group.

Chapter 3: Teaching Reading Comprehension: *Introduction*

This chapter takes a close look at what proficient readers do automatically when they read and how teachers can help less-proficient readers do the same. These reading comprehension strategies will include predicting and making connections, asking questions of oneself and the author, clarifying for meaning, and summarizing the main ideas from the reading.

What are the specific reading comprehension strategies?

This chapter begins with identifying the specific strategies that good readers use independently, automatically, and quickly.

1. **PREDICT**
2. **DETERMINE THE MOST IMPORTANT IDEAS AND THEMES**
3. **CLARIFY AND ASK QUESTIONS OF THEMSELVES AND THE AUTHOR**
4. **USE PRIOR KNOWLEDGE**
5. **SUMMARIZE**
6. **CREATE VISUAL IMAGES**
7. **USE FIX-UP STRATEGIES**

Chapter 3 focuses on the following:

- Using prediction to make connections
- Making connections to self, world, and other books
- Using questioning for reading comprehension
- Using summarizing for reading comprehension
- Using graphic organizers for reading comprehension

Each section of this chapter provides the following:

- An activity to teach and to model the strategy explicitly
- An example of the activity to teach the strategy
- Practice exercises

Chapter 3: Teaching Reading Comprehension: *What Proficient Readers Do*

Use the following ideas to teach these strategies to your students.

- ◆ **Proficient readers think about their own thinking during reading.**
  - model
  - think aloud as you read
  - use specific reading terminology with students
  - expect students to use specific reading terminology

- ◆ **Proficient readers know when they do comprehend and when they do not comprehend.**
  - help students chunk information and focus their attention on chunks of text at a time
  - encourage students to use graphic organizers
  - work collaboratively

- ◆ **Proficient readers can identify their purposes for reading in different types of texts.**
  - model
  - think aloud as you read
  - provide opportunities for students to read and research a variety of texts
  - invite students to write for a variety of purposes

- ◆ **Proficient readers know when and why the meaning of a text is unclear to them.**
  - model
  - think aloud
  - teach students to generate their own questions
  - provide opportunities for students to dialogue about their reading

- ◆ **Proficient readers use a variety of strategies to solve comprehension problems.**
  - model
  - think aloud
  - teach specific strategies of what to do when they don't know the meaning of a word
  - teach specific strategies of what to do when they don't understand something they have read

Chapter 3: Teaching Reading Comprehension: *Using Predictions to Make Connections*

It is important to begin strategy instruction with texts that are close to the students' own experiences. This allows the students to learn new ways to think about their reading. When children have heard and read an extensive array of narrative and expository texts, they stretch and begin to make connections between books and their lives. They can then begin to make connections from what they read to the world. Now they are ready to think about and read about more challenging issues and themes.

Strategy Lesson Plan 1: As part of a readers' workshop, provide focus lessons on the three different types of connections readers make: text-to-self, text-to-text, text-to-world.

Although there are a variety of formats for a readers' workshop, the following variation is very effective.

Silent Sustained Reading - 10–20 minutes. During this time the teacher can hold reading conferences with students. These conferences can be used to teach or reinforce a specific reading strategy, listen to a student read, check for comprehension with a retell, or find out more about the student's attitude and habits of reading. (Remember to give students a specific purpose before reading.)

Focus Lesson - 5–15 minutes. During this time the teacher works with the whole group to introduce, model, teach, and/or record the students' thinking and understanding of specific skills and reading strategies.

Workshop - 25–40 minutes. During this time the teacher does guided instruction with small groups of students for literature study, reciprocal teaching, or special needs groups.

Sharing - 5–10 minutes. During this time students share with the whole group their literature responses, questions, observations, or favorite passages.

*Provide opportunities for students to share with the class what strategies they use.

** **Teachers need to use authentic and challenging texts (high quality literature and well-written nonfiction) to help their students move from novice to professional readers.**

Name: _____ Date: _____

Chapter 3: Teaching Reading Comprehension: *Using Predictions to Make Connections*

Strategy Lesson Plan 2: Predicting

Student Directions: As you read, pay close attention to the parts of the text where you find yourself making a prediction. Using the form below, jot down the first and last word of the passage or identify the picture that helped you make a prediction. Then write down your prediction. When you have finished your reading, go back and check to see if your predictions actually happened. Then write down what really happened.

Passage or Picture: _____

Prediction: _____

_____

Was your prediction right? _____ If not, what did happen? _____

_____

Passage or Picture: _____

Prediction: _____

_____

Was your prediction right? _____ If not, what did happen? _____

_____

Passage or Picture: _____

Prediction: _____

_____

Was your prediction right? _____ If not, what did happen? _____

_____

Name: _____ Date: _____

Chapter 3: Teaching Reading Comprehension: *Using Predictions to Make Connections (continued)*

Strategy Lesson Plan 3: Making Connections

Student Directions: As you read, pay close attention to the parts of the text where you find yourself making **a connection to your own life**. Using the form below, jot down the first and last word of the passage or identify the picture where you made the connection to your life. Then write down your connection.

Passage or Picture: _____

_____

Connection to My Life: _____

_____

_____

_____

_____

Passage or Picture: _____

_____

Connection to My Life: _____

_____

_____

_____

_____

Name: _____   Date: _____

Chapter 3: Teaching Reading Comprehension: *Using Predictions to Make Connections (continued)*

Strategy Lesson Plan 4: Making Connections

Student Directions: As you read, pay close attention to the parts of the text where you find yourself making **a connection to another text that you have read**. Using the form below, jot down the first and last word of the passage or identify the picture where you made the connection to another text. Then write down your connection.

Passage or Picture: _____

_____

Connection to Another Text I've Read: _____

_____

_____

_____

_____

Passage or Picture: _____

_____

Connection to Another Text I've Read: _____

_____

_____

_____

_____

Name: _____   Date: _____

Chapter 3: Teaching Reading Comprehension: *Using Predictions to Make Connections (continued)*

Strategy Lesson Plan 5: Making Connections

Student Directions: As you read, pay close attention to the parts of the text where you find yourself making **a connection to other knowledge you have about the world.** Using the form below, jot down the first and last word of the passage or identify the picture where you made the connection to other knowledge. Then write down your connection.

Passage or Picture: _____

_____

Connection to the World: _____

_____

_____

_____

_____

Passage or Picture: _____

_____

Connection to the World: _____

_____

_____

_____

_____

Name: _____ Date: _____

Chapter 3: Teaching Reading Comprehension: *Practice Making Connections (Example)*

Jeremy

Jeremy woke up to the sound of rain. It was still dark, but he could hear his mother down in the kitchen. He could smell the kerosene of the lit lamp. Sliding out of bed slowly, he made sure he did not wake Billy. His younger brother had been ill with a fever for several days. Jeremy tucked the quilt just under Billy's chin. He then climbed down the ladder steps to the kitchen.

His mother was tending the fire in the stove. Jeremy filled a small cooking pot with water and placed it on the stove to boil for the porridge. He fanned the fire as his mother measured the oatmeal. Neither of them spoke. The sound of rain on the roof seemed to pound harder and harder. Finally, he asked, "Should I wake Sarah and Grace?"

"Not just yet," his mother replied. "Wait until you've fed the livestock."

Jeremy took a faded, worn jacket from a corner wall hook and left the house. As he walked to the barn, he pulled the collar of the oversized jacket over his face. Every morning it was the same. He hoped to smell the familiar scent of his father, but it, like the jacket, had faded with time. Opening the barn door, he wished he could accompany his father once again to the barn early on a rainy morning. The cows were mooing softly in anticipation of their breakfast and milking. His father had loved this time in the morning.

Regretting the times he had slept late while his father did the chores, he moved quickly to finish his morning duties. Jeremy wanted to say, "Don't worry, Dad, I can take care of the family."

Back in the kitchen, Sarah and Grace had hurriedly dressed in front of the warm fire and were now eating breakfast. Jeremy would walk his sisters to school as he always had, but now, instead of joining them in their one-room schoolhouse, he would return home to help his mother. There was much to do to prepare for harvest.

Name: _____   Date: _____

Chapter 3: Teaching Reading Comprehension: *Practice Making Connections (Example)*

Student Directions: As you read, pay close attention to the parts of the text where you find yourself making **a connection to your own life**. Using the form below, jot down the first and last word of the passage or identify the picture where you made the connection to your life. Then write down your connection.

Passage or Picture:

"The sound of rain … harder."

Connection to My Life:

My grandma has a tin roof. Whenever I sleep at her house, I stay in a room upstairs. When it rains, the pounding on the roof keeps me awake.

Now You Practice

Passage or Picture: _____

_____

Connection to My Life: _____

_____

_____

_____

_____

_____

_____

_____

_____

Name: _____   Date: _____

Chapter 3: Teaching Reading Comprehension: *Practice Making Connections (Example)*

Student Directions: As you read, pay close attention to the parts of the text where you find yourself making **a connection to another text that you have read**. Using the form below, jot down the first and last word of the passage or identify the picture where you made the connection to another text. Then write down your connection.

Passage or Picture:

"He then climbed … kitchen."

Connection to Another Text I've Read:

That reminds me of the <u>Little House on the Prairie</u> books. I loved reading about living in the olden days without electricity. I don't think I could do all those chores.

Now You Practice

Passage or Picture: _____

_____

Connection to Another Text I've Read: _____

_____

_____

_____

_____

_____

_____

_____

_____

Name: _____ Date: _____

Chapter 3: Teaching Reading Comprehension: *Practice Making Connections (Example)*

Student Directions: As you read, pay close attention to the parts of the text where you find yourself making **a connection to other knowledge you have about the world**. Using the form below, jot down the first and last word of the passage or identify the picture where you made the connection to other knowledge. Then write down your connection.

Passage or Picture:

"Jeremy would walk … mother."

Connection to the World:

Today children have to stay in school until they are sixteen.
It is the law. It is kind of sad that he couldn't go back to school. I wonder if he will ever get to go back to school.

Now You Practice

Passage or Picture: _____

_____

Connection to the World: _____

_____

_____

_____

_____

_____

_____

_____

Chapter 3: Teaching Reading Comprehension: *Using Questioning for Comprehension*

Teacher Focus:

Questions are the keys to understanding what one reads. Questioning makes it possible to clarify any confusion, and comprehension is the absence of confusion. Brain research shows that the brain seeks to make meaning. Children as readers want desperately to make meaning of what they read and of what is happening in their world. Questions take us deeper into understanding.

Proficient readers question constantly without realizing. Children who are learning to read or reading to learn often don't know that. They think their questions mean they are not good readers. That is why teachers must tell students and model with them that their questions are important. When readers have questions and seek the answers, they are monitoring their reading and are making meaning.

Strategy Lesson Plan 1: Whole-class discussion about the importance of questioning when one reads. *(This lesson can be divided into two or more focus lessons.)*

- Model with students using an adult text you have recently read.

- Place question marks beside the places in the text where you had a question. Show an overhead of this page to the students.

- Share the questions you had BEFORE, DURING, AND AFTER your reading.

- Scribe your questions on an overhead or flip chart.

- Follow up with a group discussion identifying what type of questions you had.

  * Questions that can be answered explicitly from the information in the text

  * Questions that can be answered by putting together different pieces of information found in the text

  * Questions whose answers can be inferred from the text and your own prior knowledge

  * Questions that can be answered by further discussion or research

  * Questions that cannot be answered

- Provide opportunities for students to use their own reading and identify their own types of questions.

Name: _____ Date: _____

Chapter 3: Teaching Reading Comprehension: *Questioning*

Student Directions: As you read, stop and think about the questions you have. Good readers ask questions **BEFORE** they read, **DURING** their reading, and **AFTER** they read. Highlight or tab with a sticky note where you have questions, then record those questions in the following boxes. Also record any answers to your questions that you discover. You can do this during your reading or after you have finished reading.

Questions I Have Before I Read

   1. _____

   2. _____

   3. _____

Any Answers? _____

_____

Questions I Have During My Reading

   1. _____

   2. _____

   3. _____

Any Answers? _____

_____

Questions I Have After I Read

   1. _____

   2. _____

   3. _____

Any Answers? _____

_____

Name: _____ Date: _____

Chapter 3: Teaching Reading Comprehension: *Practice Questioning (Example)*

Student Reminder: Remember, these are the **question words** to ask as you read.

WHO?	**WHEN?**	**WHY?**
WHAT?	**WHERE?**	**HOW?**

The Ocean's Mystery

There are many mysteries hidden in the depths of the ocean. One of these mysteries is a creature that no one has ever seen alive, and it lives in the unexplored darkness of the ocean floor. Over the centuries, stories have been told of colossal sea monsters that have risen from the ocean to attack ships at sea. Although many of these stories are products of imagination, there is one ocean creature that is known to have attacked ships. This awesome sea creature is the giant squid.

There has been clear evidence of the existence of the giant squid. Carcasses of giant squid have washed ashore on many occasions. There have also been many factual reports of terrible attacks on ships. Jules Vern used some of those reports for scenes in his book *20,000 Leagues Under the Sea*. Strangely, no human being has seen a living giant squid in its own natural environment.

The size of a giant squid is estimated between 60 and 75 feet. It can weigh more than a ton. The eyes are between 18 and 20 inches in diameter. The giant squid uses its two elongated tentacles to snare its prey. The tentacles have sharp-toothed suckers that draw its prey to its sharp beak and tongue.

The giant squid's natural enemy is the sperm whale. Researchers watch for the feeding grounds of the sperm whale in the hopes of being the first to witness an encounter between these two giants of the ocean.

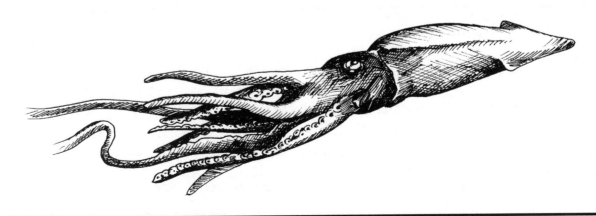

Name: _____ Date: _____

Chapter 3: Teaching Reading Comprehension: *Practice Questioning (Example)*

Student Directions: As you read, stop and think about the questions you have. Good readers ask questions **BEFORE** they read, **DURING** their reading, and **AFTER** they read. Highlight or tab with a sticky note where you have questions, then record those questions in the following boxes. Also record any answers to your questions that you discover. You can do this during your reading or after you have finished reading.

Questions I Have Before I Read

1. *What is the ocean's mystery?*

2. _____

3. _____

Any Answers? *No one has ever really seen a giant squid alive.*

Questions I Have During My Reading

1. *Why haven't people seen the giant squid alive?*

2. *Where have they found the squids' carcasses?*

3. _____

Any Answers? *I'll have to read more about giant squid to find out. I think the best way to see the giant squid alive is to search the ocean area where a carcass comes ashore.*

Questions I Have After I Read

1. *How does the sperm whale kill a giant squid?*

2. *What exactly are the researchers doing to find the giant squid?*

3. _____

Any Answers? *I don't know. I'll have to do more research or ask someone.*

Name: _____ Date: _____

Chapter 3: Teaching Reading Comprehension: *Now You Practice Questioning*

The Mystery of the Wildman of China

There are many stories of a large, human-like creature living in the forests of the Chinese mountains. In 1976 a group of Chinese loggers was traveling by truck on a dirt road through the forest in the valley of the Chang River. Suddenly, standing in the middle of the road was a large, hairy creature. The driver slammed on his brakes. A few of the men cautiously approached the creature, but it abruptly turned and disappeared into the trees and undergrowth.

What they saw was not like any other forest creature they had seen before. They decided it must have been a Wildman. There had been many tales about the "Wildman" told by their forefathers through the centuries. The loggers reported to the Chinese Academy of Sciences that they had seen a tall, heavily built creature covered with hair.

After this sighting in 1976, there were more reports of sightings of Wildmen from the same region of the country. A team of 100 scientific experts and the Chinese army worked over two years searching the thick forest of that region. Over 500 square miles were searched. Local people in the area described many sightings.

One amazing report came from Pang Gensheng. He had been chopping wood when a Wildman approached him. Frightened, he backed up until he stood at the edge of a cliff. With nowhere to go, he raised his ax at the creature. The Wildman stopped, and the two stared at each other for an hour. Finally, Gensheng reached down, picked up a rock, and threw it at the creature. It howled in pain and ran off. Gensheng reported that the Wildman had been about seven feet tall with wide shoulders, sloping forehead, and long arms.

Although there is no conclusive proof, there are many scientists who are convinced that the Wildman of China and other wild man-like creatures exist in unexplored parts of the world. The search goes on.

Name: _____   Date: _____

Chapter 3: Teaching Reading Comprehension: *Now You Practice Questioning (continued)*

Student Directions: As you read, stop and think about the questions you have. Good readers ask questions **BEFORE** they read, **DURING** their reading, and **AFTER** they read. Highlight or tab with a sticky note where you have questions, then record those questions in the following boxes. Also record any answers to your questions that you discover. You can do this during your reading or after you have finished reading.

Questions I Have Before I Read

1. _____

2. _____

3. _____

Any Answers? _____

_____

Questions I Have During My Reading

1. _____

2. _____

3. _____

Any Answers? _____

_____

Questions I Have After I Read

1. _____

2. _____

3. _____

Any Answers? _____

_____

Chapter 3: Teaching Reading Comprehension: *Using Graphic Organizers to Clarify*

When students read different kinds of reading passages, it helps to create a visual graphic organizer. Working with graphic organizers in reading and writing allows students to highlight the important parts of what they are reading. Students can then "see" this information, and it helps them to carry meaning as they read. In turn, the student will be better able to clarify when meaning gets blurred.

There are many different types of graphic organizers that can help students organize information as they read. When using graphic organizers to teach reading comprehension, it is important to plan specifically what reading strategy you are teaching or reinforcing. It is even more important that your students know why they are doing the graphic organizer. They need to be able to articulate what reading strategies they are using.

Example: K-W-L Charts *(Know-Want-Learn)*

Purpose: To activate prior knowledge, to generate questions, and to identify main ideas and themes.

What I know	What I want to know	What I learned
1.	1.	1.
2.	2.	2.
3.	3.	3.

Name: _____ Date: _____

Chapter 3: Teaching Reading Comprehension: *Graphic Organizer Practice 1*

Practice: Read the article beginning on page 44 and use the graphic organizers to keep track of the most important information.

I. BEFORE YOU READ

Read the title of the article and the first paragraph.
1. What part of Egypt's history does this article describe?

_____

_____

2. Preview the article by looking at any photographs or illustrations. Read any captions that go with the pictures.
3. What do the pictures tell you about this part of the world? Choose two pictures and record your ideas.

The picture of	tells me...

The picture of	tells me...

Name: _____ Date: _____

Chapter 3: Teaching Reading Comprehension: *Graphic Organizer Practice 1 (continued)*

II. WHILE YOU READ

1. Use the graphic organizer to keep track of the details about Hatshepsut, an Egyptian queen.

2. Record information that seems important and any questions that you have as you read.

Main Idea
The Egyptian queen Hatshepsut was one of the greatest women in the history of the world.

Name: _____ Date: _____

Chapter 3: Teaching Reading Comprehension: *Graphic Organizer Practice 1 (continued)*

Egypt's Queen Hatshepsut

The history of Egypt has fascinated people for centuries. Egypt stands at a crossroads that links the three continents of Africa, Asia, and Europe. One of the most fascinating things about Egypt's history is the role of women. There were many Egyptian queens who were significant to Egypt's political success. Hatshepsut, the daughter of a great warrior-king, became the third woman pharaoh in Egypt's history.

In 1500 B.C. Hatshepsut, whose name means "most noble of all women," was in her teens. She was the only daughter of King Thutmose and his royal wife Ahmose. Only men were supposed to rule. Hatshepsut's father arranged for her to be married. Unfortunately, she became a young widow with one young daughter and one infant son. Upon the death of her father and husband, she then had an empire to rule. Never before had Egypt ruled such a huge territory. The empire expanded far into Asia and south into regions of Africa. Egypt was a wealthy land that was rich in natural resources and bountiful crops.

With her son an infant, Hatshepsut was the only adult in the royal family who could rule. The queen enjoyed the challenge of leading the government. She decided not to remarry. After a few years, she believed that with all the responsibilities of ruling the country, she also deserved the title of ruler. She proclaimed herself the legal king and made preparations for her daughter to succeed her to the throne.

Stop and Think

Summarize:

What do you know about Hatshepsut? How did she become ruler of Egypt? Jot down **a few words** in the first column of your graphic organizer to tell the main points so far.
(Remember, good readers summarize as they read.)

Name: _____ Date: _____

Chapter 3: Teaching Reading Comprehension: *Graphic Organizer Practice 1 (continued)*

Clarify:

Jot down one word that you are not sure of the meaning. Be sure to include what you think it might mean, and why you think that may be the meaning.

Word: _____ I think it means _____

_____

because _____

_____

Egypt was a wealthy country. Hatshepsut went about taking care of the internal affairs of her empire. She ordered that old temples be restored and new ones be built across the Nile Valley. The most famous new temple was known as Deir el Bahri. This was to be Hatshepsut's funeral temple. Hatshepsut also sent many trading expeditions to distant lands to trade for ivory, rare woods, and other exquisite goods.

Even though Hatshepsut led the country well, it was still unusual for a woman to rule. A king of Egypt was believed to be a son of the king of the gods. Hatshepsut proclaimed that she was "the daughter of the king of the gods, Amun-Re." She had the walls of her temples display her divinity. Hatshepsut also reminded her people of the support her father, King Thutmose, had given her when he lived. She proclaimed that he would have wanted her to succeed him as ruler of Egypt. In every way she could she linked herself with her father's name. She even built a new memorial temple within her funeral temple and reburied him there.

Stop and Think

Summarize:

What were some of Hatshepsut's accomplishments? Why did she proclaim herself "daughter of Amun-Re"? Jot down **a few words** in the second column of your graphic organizer to summarize the main points in this chunk of reading.
(Remember, good readers summarize as they read.)

45

Name: _____ Date: _____

Chapter 3: Teaching Reading Comprehension: *Graphic Organizer Practice 1 (continued)*

Question:

Jot down one question that your teacher might ask you on a quiz about this chunk of reading. *(Remember, good readers ask questions as they read.)*

_____

_____

Answer: _____

_____

> Hatshepsut proved to be a good leader in every way. She gained the respect of her father's supporters, who served her loyally. She also had talented architects and craftsmen who oversaw all the royal construction across Egypt. There were a few of Egypt's conquered territories who believed that having a woman on the throne would make it easier for them to break away from Egypt's rule. They were wrong. Hatshepsut was not afraid of going into battle herself. She was pictured on many walls of temples crushing her enemies. She was a powerful ruler indeed.

Stop and Think

Summarize:

In what ways did Hatshepsut prove her leadership skills? Jot down **a few words** in the third column of your graphic organizer to summarize the main points in this chunk of reading. *(Remember, good readers summarize as they read.)*

Predict:

Jot down a prediction before you read the end of this article.
*(Remember, good readers **predict throughout their reading**, not just at the beginning of their reading.)*

_____

_____

_____

_____

Name: _____ Date: _____

Chapter 3: Teaching Reading Comprehension: *Graphic Organizer Practice 1 (continued)*

Unfortunately, Hatshepsut's wish that her daughter would succeed her to the throne did not happen. Her daughter died, and her son, Thutmose III, eventually became king while Hatshepsut was still alive. He was put in command of the army and became a powerful military leader. His successful leadership ensured that the great Egyptian Empire would dominate the known world for more than two centuries.

Twenty years after Hatshepsut died, Thutmose III attempted to destroy all of her monuments and any evidence of her as a reigning queen of Egypt. Fortunately, there are enough records remaining that prove she was one of the most powerful women in all of Egypt's history.

Stop and Think

Summarize:

What additional information do you know about Hatshepsut? Jot down **a few words** in the fourth column to summarize the most important information in this last chunk of reading. *(Remember, good readers summarize as they read, as well as at the end of their reading.)*

Name: _____ Date: _____

Chapter 3: Teaching Reading Comprehension: *Graphic Organizer Practice 1 (continued)*

III.   AFTER YOU READ

Create a Graphic Organizer to Write a Summary:

How do you summarize the main points of the article? Follow a plan (graphic organizer). You will be successful every time!

First: Find the main idea. A summary first clearly states the main idea. Look back at your beginning graphic organizer that you added to as you read chunks of the article. Put the **main idea** in your own words and write it in the following box:

Main Idea

Second: Add supporting points and details.

How Hatshepsut became queen
Examples of her accomplishments and power
How her reign as queen ended

Closing: Rephrase the author's main point and add a concluding sentence that "clinches it" (brings it all together in an interesting way).

Closing

48

Name: _____ Date: _____

Chapter 3: Teaching Reading Comprehension: *Graphic Organizer Practice 2*

Practice 2: Read the article beginning on page 51 about the history of the calendar and use the graphic organizers to keep track of the most important information.

I. BEFORE YOU READ

Read the title of the article and the first paragraph.

Stop/Think/Predict

1. What do you think this article will explain?

   _____

   _____

   _____

2. Preview the article by looking at any photographs or illustrations.

3. What information does the picture clarify for you? Record your ideas.

The picture of	tells me…

Name: _____ Date: _____

Chapter 3: Teaching Reading Comprehension: *Graphic Organizer Practice 2 (continued)*

II. WHILE YOU READ

1. Use the graphic organizer to keep track of the details about the history of the calendar.

2. Record information that seems important and any questions that you have as you read.

Identify Main Idea
How did the Egyptian people come to create a calendar?
What problem did the people have when they developed the calendar?
What attempts did they make to solve the problem?
How did they solve the problem?

50

Name: _____ Date: _____

Chapter 3: Teaching Reading Comprehension: *Graphic Organizer Practice 2 (continued)*

Losing Days

When is your next basketball game? What date is the school play this year? What is the last day of school? When is Uncle Joe's birthday? To answer all these questions and many others each day, we refer to a calendar to help. We know we will see the 365 days of the year (366 days in a leap year) divided into 12 months. Where did that calendar come from?

For centuries the Egyptian farmers could depend on the yearly flooding of the Nile River. They knew how to plan for it and how to take advantage of it. They would move their livestock to higher lands and prepare to catch the water in reservoirs to be used during times of drought. The farmers also planned to plant their crops in the rich soil after the flood.

The Egyptian people watched the stars carefully to mark the passing of time. In 3,000 B.C., many Egyptian astronomers noticed that the bright star Sirius appeared for an instant on the horizon just before the sun came up in the morning. This appearance of Sirius happened only once every year, and it marked the beginning of flood season. Based on the appearance of Sirius, the Egyptian astronomers created a 365-day calendar. The year was divided into 12 months, each with 30 days. This calendar left five extra days at the end of the year. These five days became special holidays that marked festivals honoring their gods.

Stop and Think

Summarize:

What do you know about how we got the calendar we use today? Jot down **a few words** in the first block of your graphic organizer to tell the main points so far.
(Remember, good readers summarize as they read.)

Name: _____ Date: _____

Chapter 3: Teaching Reading Comprehension: *Graphic Organizer Practice 2 (continued)*

Clarify:

Jot down **one word** that you are not sure of the meaning. Be sure to include what you think it might mean, and why you think that may be the meaning.

Word: _____

I think it means _____

_____

because _____

_____

The Egyptian calendar with 365 days had a problem. It was shorter than the solar year by almost one-fourth of a day. After a time, the days and months of the year were happening at the wrong time of year. The Egyptian farmers stopped using the calendar and again watched for the appearance of Sirius once a year in the morning sky.

During this same time, the Romans had a lunar calendar that was based on the phases of the moon. The Roman months went from one new moon to the next new moon. That meant that each month had about $29\frac{1}{2}$ days. The Romans' calendar problem was similar to that of the Egyptians'. By the time Julius Caesar came to rule Rome, not one month was falling in the right season. The Roman calendar was 80 days behind the solar year.

Stop and Think

Summarize:

What was the problem with Egypt's calendar? What similar problem did Italy have? Jot down **a few words** in the second block of your graphic organizer to summarize the main points in this chunk of reading.

(Remember, good readers summarize as they read.)

Name: _____ Date: _____

Chapter 3: Teaching Reading Comprehension: *Graphic Organizer Practice 2 (continued)*

Question:

Jot down **one question** that your teacher might ask you on a quiz about this chunk of the reading.
(Remember, good readers ask questions as they read.)

_____

_____

Answer: _____

_____

Caesar had the Greek astronomer Sosigenes develop a solar calendar like the Egyptians, but the new calendar would make the seasons and the calendar work together. Caesar added the 80 extra days to the 365 days of the Egyptian calendar. He then declared that the Roman year 709 would be 445 days long. This made the Roman calendar match the solar year.

This new Roman calendar was named the Julian calendar, after Julius Caesar. It began on January 1st with half of the months having 30 days and the other half having 31. To make the numbers equal 365, Sosigenes took one day out of the month of February. To make sure the calendar remained accurate over time, he planned a "leap" every four years and added a day to the month of February.

Stop and Think

Summarize:

How did Julius Caesar try to solve the problem? Jot down **a few words** in the third block of your graphic organizer to summarize the main points in this chunk of reading.
(Remember, good readers summarize as they read.)

Predict:

Jot down a prediction before you read the end of this article.
*(Remember, good readers **predict throughout their reading**, not just at the beginning of their reading.)*

_____

_____

Name: _____ Date: _____

Chapter 3: Teaching Reading Comprehension: *Graphic Organizer Practice 2 (continued)*

The new Julian calendar worked well because the solar year is almost $365\frac{1}{4}$ days. Almost, but not exactly! The Julian calendar year was approximately 11 minutes longer than the solar year. By the late 1500s, the Julian calendar was almost ten days too long. This was of special concern to those who practiced the Christian faith, because Easter was supposed to be connected to the first day of spring in the solar year. The ten-day discrepancy in the calendar made it seem that the first day of spring was occurring too soon.

In 1582, Pope Gregory XIII worked with the German astronomer Christopher Clavius to solve the problem. Pope Gregory made two specific changes. First, he eliminated a few leap years. Then he announced that October 4, 1582, would be followed by October 15, 1582. This took care of the ten-day difference between the calendar year and the solar year. This new calendar was called the Gregorian calendar.

We still use the Gregorian calendar. Because it matches the solar year almost exactly, we don't have to worry about "losing days" of our lives.

Stop and Think

Summarize:

How was the problem with the Julian calendar solved? Jot down **a few words** in the fourth column to tell the most important information in this last chunk of reading.
(Remember, good readers summarize as they read, as well as at the end of their reading.)

Name: _____ Date: _____

Chapter 3: Teaching Reading Comprehension: *Graphic Organizer Practice 2 (continued)*

III. AFTER YOU READ

Create a Graphic Organizer to Write a Summary:

How do you summarize the main points of the article? Follow a plan (graphic organizer). You will be successful every time!

First: Identify the problem described in the article. A summary first clearly states the main idea (problem). Look back at your beginning graphic organizer that you added to as you read chunks of the article. Put the **main idea identifying the problem** in your own words and write it in the following box:

Problem

Who _____

What _____

Why _____

Second: Add supporting points and details.

Solution

Attempted Solutions	Results
1. _____	1. _____
_____	_____
2. _____	2. _____
_____	_____
3. _____	3. _____
_____	_____

End Result

Name: _____ Date: _____

Chapter 3: Teaching Reading Comprehension: *Graphic Organizer Practice 2 (continued)*

Closing: Rephrase the author's main point and add a concluding sentence that "clinches it" (brings it all together in an interesting way).

┌───┐
│   **Closing**   │
│   │
│   │
│   │
│   │
│   │
└───┘

Stop and Write

Now that you have completed the thinking necessary for good comprehension, you are ready to write a summary. Use your problem/solution graphic organizer to write a one-paragraph summary.

_____

_____

_____

_____

_____

_____

_____

_____

_____

_____

Chapter 4: Comprehending Narrative and Expository Texts: *Narrative Reading Passages*

Narrative texts are fiction. They are made up from someone's imagination. We all enjoy a good story that makes us laugh, makes us cry, scares us, or makes us think.

Identifying the Elements of a Narrative Story

Setting is where and when the story takes place. Sometimes the author doesn't say exactly when or where the story takes place. He will give clues like the kind of clothes the characters are wearing or a description of what the place looks like to help you know the time and place.

Characters are players in the story. Story characters can be people, animals, and sometimes objects. As you read, notice the ways in which the author describes how they look, how they act, how they think, and how they change.

Plot is what events take place in the story. There is usually a big problem in the story. The characters have to work to solve the conflict.

Theme is the message of the story. It is the lesson we learned from reading the story. It is the most important idea of the story.

Remember as you read to keep asking questions.

- Who are the main characters? What do I know about them?

- Where is the story taking place?

- When is the story taking place?

- What is the problem? What is happening? What is the sequence of events?

- What is the theme? What does the author want me to learn?

Name: _____　Date: _____

Chapter 4: Comprehending Narrative and Expository Texts: *Narrative Reading Practice—Sequence Map*

Directions: Read the following narrative story and keep track of the story elements by asking yourself and the author questions.

To keep track of the plot, it can be useful to keep a sequence map as you read. Use the following graphic organizer to practice sequencing as you read *It Couldn't Be!*

Sequence Map

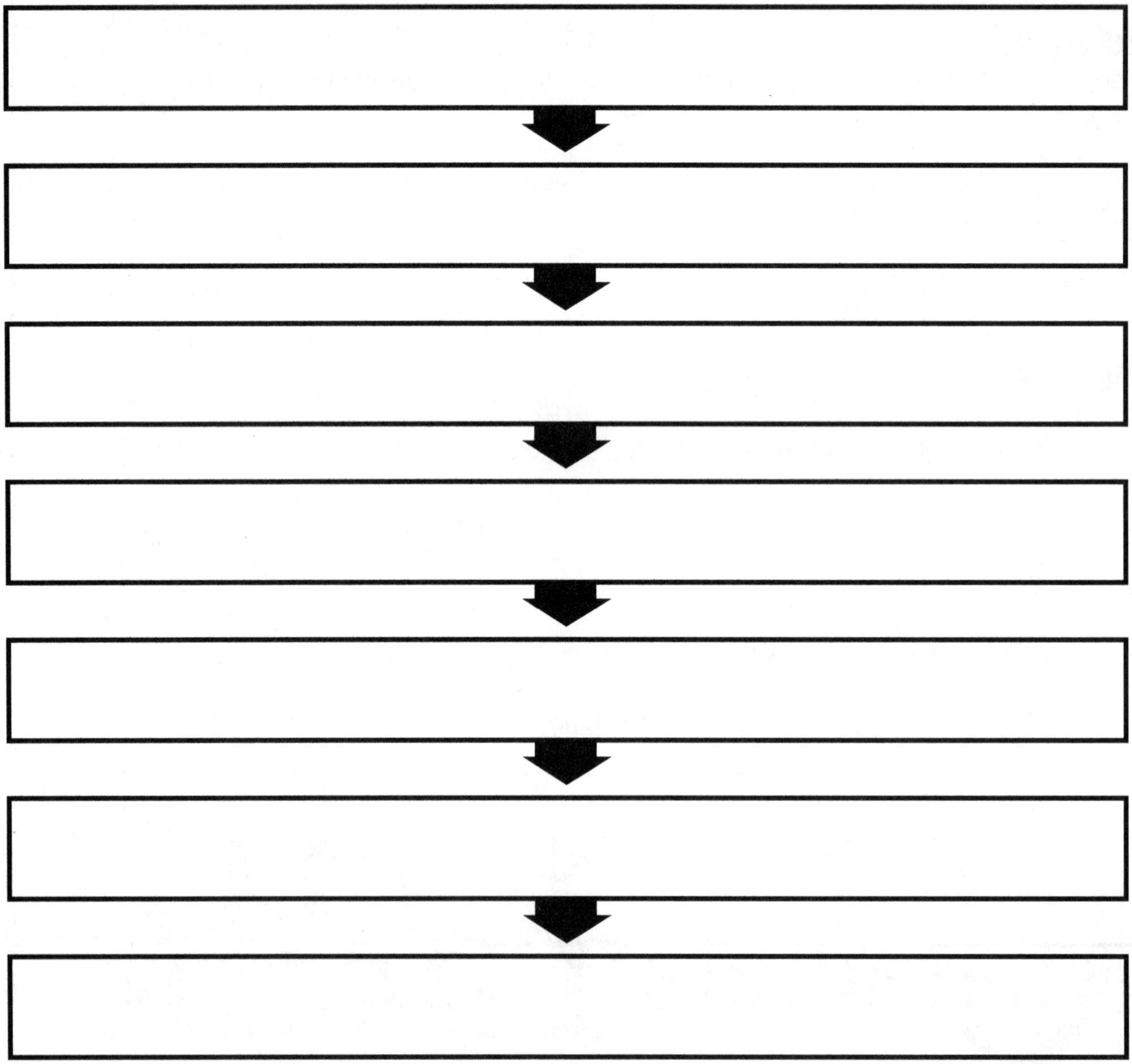

Name: _____   Date: _____

Chapter 4: Comprehending Narrative and Expository Texts: *Narrative Reading Practice (continued)*

It Couldn't Be!

"It wasn't my idea to move to Missouri! Why did I have to try to find something good about this dreary place? There wasn't anything at all "good" about the town, the kids at school, or this run-down farmhouse. I don't like it now, and I will never like it." That's what I wanted to scream at my mom when she tried to convince me that our new home outside of Fulton, Missouri, was a wonderful place. Instead, I just stared at the wall, avoiding eye contact with her.

"Megan, please try," my mom urged one last time.

When Dad decided to leave the military and go into business for himself, everybody in the family was excited about the possibilities. I had no idea that meant moving from Oklahoma to another state and leaving all my friends, especially Sara. We had been best friends since first grade. I just knew I would never have another friend like her. Sara had always been there when I needed to talk. We shared everything and went everywhere together.

Days passed. It was exactly as I thought it would be. Boring and awful! My teacher, Miss Ramus, was strict and demanding. She never smiled. The school was old and dilapidated. It didn't even have a real gym. Worst of all, my classmates seemed to ignore me. Each day when I got to school, I went immediately to my room and waited for the bell to ring. When school was out, I hurriedly got my books from my locker and headed for the bus, hoping I could get a seat in the front close to the bus driver.

I was not quick enough on Friday of the third week. I had to stay and get a missed math assignment from Miss Ramus. When I got to the bus, all the front seats were full. As I sulked toward the back of the bus hoping to find a seat by myself, I felt a tug at my sleeve. "Megan, why don't you sit here with me?"

Name: _____ Date: _____

Chapter 4: Comprehending Narrative and Expository Texts: *Narrative Reading Practice (continued)*

It Couldn't Be! (continued)

I turned to see who had made the offering. She was a tall, pretty girl with long blonde hair pulled back in a ponytail. I thought she might have been in the classroom across the hall from me. I'd seen her on the bus and in the hallways, but I didn't know her name. "Thanks," I said as I sat down, holding my books hard against my chest, looking straight ahead, and hoping she wouldn't ask me anything.

"You know, I live just down the road from your house. In fact, from my bedroom window I can see the roof of your barn."

"Uhm." I nodded an audible response. An awkward moment passed.

"Actually, there is a path in the woods that goes from our back pasture right to your back yard. I know that because I used to visit the family who lived there at one time."

Still looking straight ahead, I nodded my head and said, "Oh!" The bus was only a few yards from my driveway. As I prepared to leave, my seat partner suddenly grabbed my hand.

"I have a great idea!" she gleefully pronounced. "I'll get off here with you. Let's ask your mom if you can walk over to my house to see our new baby calf. She was just born yesterday."

I was smiling for the first time in weeks as we got off the bus. We walked toward the house. "By the way," she said, "my name is Sara Peterson."

It couldn't be!

Name: _____ Date: _____

Chapter 4: Comprehending Narrative and Expository Texts:
Narrative Reading Practice—Story Map

Directions: Check your comprehension. Fill in the following graphic organizer.

Title: _____

Setting:

    * When _____

    * Where _____

Characters:

    * _____   * _____

    * _____   * _____

    * _____   * _____

Plot: (What are the events in order?)

    * _____

    * _____

    * _____

    * _____

    * _____

    * _____

    * _____

Theme: _____

_____

_____

_____

Chapter 4: Comprehending Narrative and Expository Texts: *Expository Reading Passages*

Expository text is **nonfiction or informational** text. The purpose of all expository reading is to give the reader information about a topic. Expository texts are written in paragraphs. Each paragraph will have a **topic sentence** that tells what information will be in the paragraph.

First: Finding the Main Idea

The main idea of an expository reading passage is the author's major point about the topic. The main idea of an informational text is often in a sentence or two at the beginning of the reading. This is called a **thesis statement.**

Second: Understanding Details

Identify the main idea and then look for **supporting details**. Ask yourself, "What **details, facts, or examples** does the author give to support the **topic sentence**?"

Strategies to Get Ready to Read

Teach your students to do the following steps **before** reading.

- PREVIEW a selection. Read the title and the first few sentences.
- USE PRIOR KNOWLEDGE. Think about what you already know about the topic.
- PREDICT what you think the next part of the reading will be about.
- ASK QUESTIONS OF YOURSELF. Think about what you want to know about the topic.

Strategies to Use During Reading

Teach your students to do the following strategies **during** their reading.

- Adjust reading rate
- Predict along the way
- Clarify confusing parts
- Question
- Reread
- Summarize along the way
- Visualize
- Use context clues when possible
- Take notes

Strategies to Use After Reading

Teach your students to do the following steps **after** reading.

- Confirm or adjust predictions
- Visualize
- Summarize
- Question
- Reread or skim back if necessary to check understanding
- Think aloud with someone
- Retell
- Take notes
- Make inferences
- Reflect

Name: _____ Date: _____

Chapter 4: Comprehending Narrative and Expository Texts: *Expository Reading Practice*

Directions: Read the following expository reading passage and look for the main idea of the passage, the topic sentence in each paragraph, and the supporting information.

Petrified Forest National Park

The Petrified Forest National Park is located in northern Arizona. It is a forest with trees made of stone. When you visit there, you will see rainbow-colored stone columns and logs where living trees once stood tall. The word petrified is defined as "turned to stone." The Petrified Forest National Park also has stone animals. These are fossils of ancient reptiles and amphibians that roamed the world centuries ago, even before the time of dinosaurs. That time was called the Triassic Period, 225 million years ago. Today the Petrified Forest is a desert, but 225 million years ago it was a lush green land with streams where strange amphibians and reptiles lived. The land was covered in thick forests of giant trees. These pine-like trees were 250 feet tall. These are the animals and trees that today make up the Petrified Forest National Park.

How could living things be turned to stone? When the trees died, they were washed away by raging flood waters into vast marshes. The trees sank to the bottom and were covered with sediment. At the same time volcanoes erupted, and tons of volcanic ash spewed out into the marshes. The ash dissolved and soaked through to the decaying trees. As the wood of the trees rotted away, it was replaced with a mineral from the volcanic ash called silica. When the marshes finally dried up, the silica hardened into quartz, which is a glass-like stone. The petrified trees are so perfect that you can see the grain of the wood as well as the trees' rings of years. The rainbow of colors comes from other minerals, such as carbon, iron, and manganese.

Name: _____ Date: _____

Chapter 4: Comprehending Narrative and Expository Texts: *Expository Reading Practice (continued)*

Directions: Fill in the following information about your reading.

First Paragraph

Topic Sentence _____

_____

Important Supporting Details

1. _____

2. _____

3. _____

4. _____

Second Paragraph

Topic Sentence _____

_____

Important Supporting Details

1. _____

2. _____

3. _____

4. _____

Name: _____   Date: _____

Chapter 4: Comprehending Narrative and Expository Texts: *Expository Reading Practice (continued)*

Directions: Continue reading the expository reading passage that follows and look for the main idea of the passage, the topic sentence in each paragraph, and the supporting information.

Petrified Forest National Park (continued)

More than 60 million years ago, pressure from the earth's inner core caused the land to bulge and form hills of sandstone, mud, and clay. These hills contained the petrified trees and animals from millions of years before. Over the years, rain, snow, and ice eroded away the soft stone. The hills were worn away, and thousands of petrified logs and fossils were unearthed.

Two thousand years later, the first people to wander into this breathtaking landscape were the Anasazi, a tribe of prehistoric American Indians. They are called the "Ancient Ones" by the Navajo Indians who live there today. The Anasazi farmed the land and built houses that were joined together to make a pueblo (village). Puerco Ruins, the finest example of an Anasazi pueblo, can be seen today as part of the Petrified Forest. The pueblo was built 900 years ago and had 75 rooms where 60 to 70 people lived. Also found at the Puerco Ruins are engravings called **petroglyphs** that show people, animals, and other mysterious symbols. The Anasazi left the Petrified Forest in search of land with more water. The Hopi Indians of Arizona and New Mexico believe that they are the descendants of the Ancient Ones.

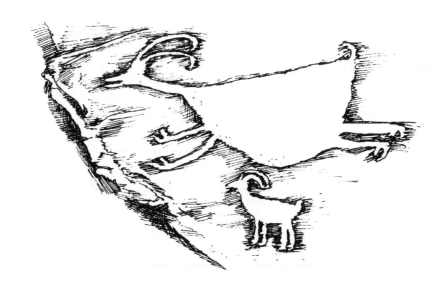

Name: _____ Date: _____

Chapter 4: Comprehending Narrative and Expository Texts: *Expository Reading Practice (continued)*

Directions: Fill in the following information about your reading.

Third Paragraph

Topic Sentence _____

_____

Important Supporting Details

1. _____

2. _____

3. _____

4. _____

Fourth Paragraph

Topic Sentence _____

_____

Important Supporting Details

1. _____

2. _____

3. _____

4. _____

Chapter 5: Answering Questions: *Introduction*

We read for many reasons.

- ♦ To enjoy a good story

- ♦ To learn about what is happening in the world around us

- ♦ To learn about a topic of interest to us

- ♦ To show we understand and comprehend what we read.

When we have to read **to show that we understand and comprehend what we read**, we usually have to answer questions. The following are different kinds of questions that we need to know how to answer:

- • Main Idea Questions

- • Detail Questions

- • Vocabulary Questions

- • Sequence Questions

- • Inference Questions

- • Theme Questions

- • Author's Point of View Questions

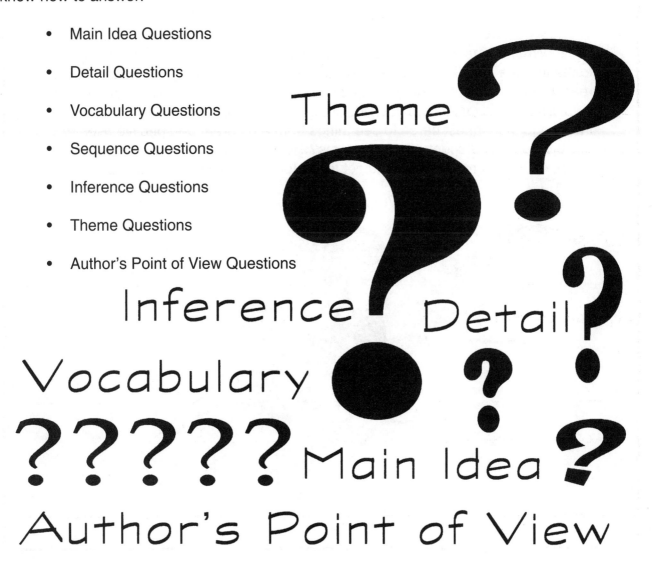

Name: _____ Date: _____

Chapter 5: Answering Questions: *Main Idea Questions*

To answer **main idea** questions, practice summarizing. Use the following steps to practice:

1. Pay close attention to the title and illustrations.
2. Read a "chunk" of material. This can be a paragraph or two.
3. Stop and try to summarize in one sentence what that "chunk" was about.
4. Read another "chunk" of material.
5. Stop and try to summarize in one sentence what that "chunk" was about.
6. Repeat this until you finish your reading.
7. Stop and try to summarize in one or two sentences what the entire reading was about.

Read the passage below and answer the **Main Idea Question**.

Defying Gravity

When someone first sees rock climbers performing fancy footwork to get to the top of a rock, he might ask, "Who would be crazy enough to do that?" The reason rock climbers climb is that it is the natural thing to do. Think about your own climbing adventures as a child. Up and onto or off furniture as a toddler. Up the tree to the highest perch to see things from a different perspective. Remember the hours you spent on jungle gyms? Rock climbers still have that youthful sense of adventure. They want to get to the top of the rock for the challenge of it.

Name: _____ Date: _____

Chapter 5: Answering Questions: *Main Idea Questions Practice*

1. What is the reading mostly about?

A.   How to become a rock climber

B.   What equipment is needed to rock climb

C.   The dangers of rock climbing

D.   Why people become rock climbers

Your answer _____

Why did you choose that answer?

_____

_____

_____

2. Why is the article called "Defying Gravity"?

A.   It shows that rock climbing can be a dangerous sport.

B.   It teaches us how to become a rock climber.

C.   It illustrates the major challenge that rock climbers face.

D.   It explains the principle of gravity.

Your answer _____

Why did you choose that answer?

_____

_____

_____

Chapter 5: Answering Questions: *Detail Questions*

To answer detail questions, pay attention to WHO, WHAT, WHEN, WHERE, WHY, and HOW questions. Remember, good readers ask questions as they read. In a narrative reading passage, make sure you know the story's setting, characters, and events. In expository reading passages, detail questions will be about supporting facts, details, and examples.

Use the following steps to practice:

1. First **scan** the reading. This means to read quickly through the passage and look for key words. Names, places, characteristics, and examples can all be important in comprehending what you have read.

2. Remember, some detail questions are answered directly in one place in the reading. At other times, you may have to put information together from two different places in the reading.

3. Pay close attention to the title and illustrations.

4. Read a "chunk" of material. This can be a paragraph or two.

5. Stop and ask who, what, when, where, why, and how questions.

6. Read another "chunk" of material.

7. Stop and ask who, what, when, where, why, and how questions.

8. Repeat this until you finish your reading.

9. Stop and ask who, what, when, where, why, and how questions.

Reading tip: Read one paragraph at a time ("chunk it") and test yourself. Cover the paragraph with your hand and try not to look back. See what you can remember.

Hint: Always pay attention to dates, names, places, and numbers.

Name: _____ Date: _____

Chapter 5: Answering Questions: *Detail Questions Practice*

Directions: Read the passage below and practice reading a chunk and then covering it. Try answering the Detail Questions after each chunk.

Defying Gravity (continued)

Rock climbing is a sport for everyone. Men, women, young, and old are all good candidates for the sport. Modern rock climbing, also called free climbing, is a simple sport. There is very little special equipment required. In fact, some people start the sport with no equipment at all. Rock climbing should not be confused with **mountaineering.** The two sports are related, but they are very different as well. Rock climbing is defined as movement over rock. Mountaineering requires movement over rock, snow, ice, and glaciers. Many skills needed for mountaineering would not likely be needed by a rock climber.

COVER THE PASSAGE

Test Yourself

1. What is another term for rock climbing? _____

2. How are rock climbing and mountaineering different?

_____

_____

_____

_____

_____

Name: _____ Date: _____

Chapter 5: Answering Questions: *Detail Questions Practice (continued)*

Defying Gravity (continued)

If you want to find out if rock climbing is a sport for you, try **bouldering**. This is the place to begin and is the most simple kind of rock climbing. All you need is yourself and a boulder big enough to climb . It is also good for training and practice for higher rock climbing. The only equipment you will need is a pair of old walking shoes or hiking boots and comfortable clothes.

Before you go in search of the perfect boulder to climb, be sure you plan to go with a partner. Never climb alone! It is also important to learn about first aid in case of any injury. Choose a boulder big enough to allow you to climb a few feet above the ground. The goal is to cross (traverse) the rock from left to right (or from right to left) without a rope. When you start practicing, remember to stay fairly close to the ground in case you slip. Bouldering will help you practice balancing abilities and using footholds and handholds. Even though you don't get very far off the ground, bouldering is a great experience that can be a test of full-fledged rock climbing skills.

COVER THE PASSAGE

Test Yourself

3. What is bouldering?

   _____

   _____

4. What equipment do you need to go bouldering?

   _____

5. What does the author recommend that you do before you try bouldering?

   _____

   _____

   _____

Chapter 5: Answering Questions: *Vocabulary Questions*

Often as we read and look for details, we encounter words that we do not know. Use the following steps to clarify vocabulary (Remember, good readers always try to clarify a word or idea they don't understand.):

1. Look at the nearby sentences for clues about the meaning of the word.

2. Analyze the word if you haven't seen it before. Do you know the root of the word? Does it have a prefix or suffix that you know? Does it look like another word that you know?

3. Look to see if there is a footnote at the end of the page that gives a definition for the word.

4. Try to substitute another word or phrase you know to see if it makes sense. (If you are taking a multiple-choice question test, substitute each of the words given as choices.)

Name: _____ Date: _____

Chapter 5: Answering Questions: *Vocabulary Questions Practice*

Read the passage below and try answering the **Vocabulary Questions.**

"Using context clues"

"Jane hated it when they fought. The yelling escalated. Jane put her hands over her ears, trying to block out the angry, hurtful words. It was no use. She couldn't smother the sounds."

If you read the passage carefully, you will have figured out what <u>escalated</u> means. The words and sentences around <u>escalated</u> help you **determine the meaning from the context of the selection.**

1. What does <u>escalated</u> mean?

   A. stopped

   B. lessened

   C. worsened

   D. flickered

"Figuring out idioms"

As the rock climber was rappelling down the 500-foot cliff, the sky opened up in a torrent of rain. It was hard to see, and the rock face was becoming slippery and treacherous. With <u>nerves of steel</u>, she calmly continued the descent and landed safely at the bottom.

2. A person with <u>nerves of steel</u> ...

   A. has great muscle strength

   B. doesn't quit when faced with difficulties

   C. is clumsy

   D. is in the best physical shape

Name: _____ Date: _____

Chapter 5: Answering Questions: *How to Make a New Word Part of Your Working Vocabulary*

WRITE ABOUT IT

Narrative Quick-Write Prompt (set timer for five minutes):

Directions: Think about a time when you or someone you knew faced difficulty with <u>nerves of steel</u>. Tell what the event was, who was involved, what happened, and how you or they reacted to the event.

_____

_____

_____

_____

_____

_____

_____

_____

_____

_____

_____

_____

_____

_____

Name: _____ Date: _____

Chapter 5: Answering Questions: *Sequence Questions Practice*

To answer sequence questions, focus on time order. Sequence questions can be asked in either narrative or expository text. Sequence questions require the reader to identify what happens in chronological order. For example, "What happened first?," "What happened next?," and "What happened last?"

To answer sequence questions, think in a "time line" as you read. Ask yourself what is happening as you read. Does it make sense?

Student Directions: Think in a "time line" as you read the following passage.

David's Wait

David's dad reached out and rustled his son's red hair. "Have a good day at school, Dave."

"Yeah, I will," David said blandly. "Bye, Mom!"

"David, don't forget your note to Miss Post!" David ran back to snatch the piece of paper off the kitchen table, and out the door he went to catch the bus.

Halfway down the block, David heard them. He knew what would come next. The older boys would begin their daily game of tormenting any younger kid waiting for the bus. David always tried to get to the bus stop just as the bus was pulling to the curb. No such luck today. Looking down Grove Avenue, David saw no sign of bus #24.

"Davey … Davey … Davey!" David recognized the taunting voice. Jack Rennard was a ninth grade bully who delighted in intimidating anyone smaller or younger than he. David didn't move as four older boys surrounded him, shoving him from one boy to the other. David held tightly to his books.

---

1. The boxes below show some of the events that took place in the passage.

1. David leaves for school.	2.	3. Jack Rennard and three other boys intimidate David at the bus stop.

What event belongs in box #2?

A. David's mom reminds him of the teacher's note.

B. David met a friend at the bus stop.

C. David holds his books tightly.

D. David's dad walks him to the bus stop.

Name: _____ Date: _____

Chapter 5: Answering Questions: *Sequence Questions Practice (continued)*

Student Directions: Read the following passage, thinking in a "time line" as you read. Then answer the question at the end of the selection.

Hey! Do You Have a Pencil?

How many times have you asked to borrow a pencil? We seem to go through so many of them, especially at school. Pencils come in a variety of colors, shapes, and lengths. The common pencil has been a part of our learning how to read and write. Pencils are tools of communication and creativity. Have you ever wondered how pencils are made?

The first step is to find the best soft wood that can hold the lead and sharpen easily. The most widely used wood is from Rocky Mountain red cedar and incense cedar trees. These trees grow mostly in the northwestern part of the United States.

The second step is making the lead that fills the center of the pencil. This material is made of water, clay, and graphite. Pencils that have harder points require graphite that contains more lead. Softer points on pencils require graphite with less lead content.

The next step is to make the lead mold by pouring the mixture of water, clay, and graphite into a long, straight string mold. This mold is forged at a high temperature and then cooled in melted wax. Then the lead strings are glued into the wood strips. After the glued lead has dried, the pencils are rubbed smooth with sandpaper and painted. Finally, the metal head holding a rubber eraser is glued on the end of each pencil.

---

2. Which of these steps is done next after the mixture of water, clay, and graphite is poured into a long, straight string mold and forged?

   A. The pencil is painted.
   B. The lead strings are glued into the wood strips.
   C. The wood is found and cut for pencils.
   D. Lead is added to the graphite to make harder points.

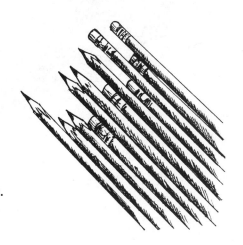

Chapter 5: Answering Questions: *Inference Questions*

To answer an **inference question**, practice putting information together. You can figure out answers to inference questions if you look for clues. You become a **reading detective**. Inference questions ask you to add your own knowledge and experience to the information in the text.

To answer inference questions, think as you read and fill in the following sentences:

"I wonder . . ."

"I think . . ."

"I'm guessing that . . ."

"I think this means . . ."

"I predict . . ."

"I believe . . ."

　　　　　　　78

Name: _____ Date: _____

Chapter 5: Answering Questions: *Inference Questions Practice*

Directions: Read the following passage and mark the places where you think you are making an inference or prediction.

The Dust Bowl

For almost a decade, the people of the American plains states faced a natural disaster. The drought hit in 1931. By 1936, there had been little precipitation. The land was scorched by the unyielding sun. Then the winds began to blow. For four years, savage dust storms destroyed the farmland, crops, and people's lives.

The region of the Dust Bowl consisted of 1,000 million acres in the panhandles of Texas and Oklahoma and parts of New Mexico, Colorado, and Kansas. The Dust Bowl was given nicknames such as "Black Blizzard" and "Black Roller" because, during the storms, a person could only see a few feet in front of him. The Dust Bowl was caused by the misuse of the land and several years of continued drought.

The wind would stir up the red, eroding, dry dirt and carry it into the sky, creating thunderclouds of swirling dust. When farmers saw the wall of desert dust, they hurriedly gathered their livestock and got them to shelter. Inside their homes, they tried to seal cracks in the walls with wet rags. The storm's dust pellets hit with such force that paint was literally sandblasted off the sides of houses.

Children had to sleep with wet towels over their faces to help filter out the dirt and sand. The lives of families were taken over with the work of cleaning up after each storm. After each storm, everyone cleaned the house, only to clean again and again. The dust, dirt, and sand buried anything not covered or under shelter. The sky could be dark for days with dust and dirt. Livestock suffered the most. Part of a child's chores each day after a dust storm was to clean the sand and dirt out of the nostrils of the livestock. Then the winds returned, and the dust would again drift like snow, covering everything in its path.

Name: _____ Date: _____

Chapter 5: Answering Questions: *Inference Questions Practice (continued)*

The Dust Bowl (continued)

Eventually hundreds of thousands of people were forced to leave their homes and their lands. Carloads of homeless and hungry men, women, and children crossed the land trying to find any work that would help them feed their families.

Has the Dust Bowl ended? The tremendous damage done by the Dust Bowl has ended. However, every year, poor agricultural practices cause more serious erosion of topsoil on the Great Plains. The winter winds can erode the loose soil from fall plowing into drifts of two to three feet deep and turn the sky dark.

---

1. What effect might the Dust Bowl have had on the children?

_____

_____

Why did you choose that answer? (Be sure you give at least two different pieces of information from your reading.)

_____

_____

2. Why was the Dust Bowl harder on farmers and their families than other people living in the Great Plains?

_____

_____

Why did you choose that answer? (Be sure you give at least two different pieces of information from your reading.)

_____

_____

Chapter 5: Answering Questions: *Theme Questions*

A story may have more than one theme. A theme is an underlying message and/or lesson that the author wants to teach, or it may be the main point of the story. Sometimes the theme has to be figured out by putting all parts of the story together. Sometimes the author tells the reader what the theme is. Think about a theme that you could apply to your own life.

Examples:

- Always be honest.

- Don't give up when things get difficult.

- Don't make fun of other people.

To answer a theme question, ask yourself the following questions:

1. What lesson can I learn from my reading?

2. What lesson does the author want me to understand?

3. What does the reading tell me about life?

4. How does the reading make me feel? Why?

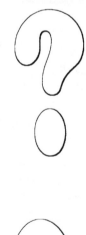

Name: _____ Date: _____

Chapter 5: Answering Questions: *Theme Questions Practice*

Directions: Read the following passage and answer the **theme question**.

Josh, B ... Gosh

Most of the guys in my class are great. Some of us are even on the same ball teams. We mess around together at recess and eat lunch together. Josh is a different story. He is a small kid and is always quiet in class. He doesn't play basketball or football. In fact, he doesn't play any sports. Actually, we don't know what he likes to do except read. Some of the guys call him a nerd.

Every October, our school has our annual Octoberfest Talent Show. Sam, Ryan, and I signed up to demonstrate our incredible basketball skills. There were categories in drama, art, sports, music, and lots of others. My friends and I thought Josh would probably enter the poetry category. We were shocked when he signed up for a comedy routine. I laughed with my friends and said, "This ought to be good!"

On the day of the talent show, my friends and I couldn't wait to see Josh flop on stage. Shy little Josh stepped on stage and paused. Was he going to say anything? I figured he was frozen with stage fright. But then ... Josh became someone else. He started with an imitation of the principal. Everyone laughed, including the principal. He then imitated other teachers. The laughter continued. Josh was really funny! He did some pantomimes of basketball players and baseball players. My friends and I were almost rolling on the floor. With a final pantomime, he stopped and bowed. Everyone applauded.

After the talent show we all thought Josh would be more outgoing and talk more, but he was just as quiet and shy as always. One thing did change, though. Josh became a welcomed addition to our lunch group. Although he didn't join us in any team sports, he was there to cheer us on and join our celebration after the game.

---

1. What lesson can we learn from this story?

   _____

   _____

2. Why did you choose that answer?

   _____

   _____

Chapter 5: Answering Questions: *Author's Point of View Questions*

Authors of nonfiction texts will have different purposes for their writing. They may be writing to inform, to teach, to persuade, and sometimes to entertain. Following are tips to discover the author's point of view and answer questions about the author's purpose.

Tips for Identifying the Author's Point of View

- **Read for word clues.** Look for positive or negative words that indicate how the author feels about the topic.

- **Read the passage carefully.** Ask yourself how the passage makes you feel. This will help you identify the author's purpose.

- **Think about the location of the nonfiction article.** Does this give you any clue as to what the author's purpose might be? Newspaper articles, magazine articles, and school textbooks may have different purposes.

Example: Read the following sentence. What is the author's point of view about french fries?

"The amount of fat and sodium present in an order of french fries makes them an unwise choice for those who are health conscience."

The author seems to think that french fries are an unhealthy food. The word *unwise* indicates a negative attitude toward french fries.

Name: _____   Date: _____

Chapter 5: Answering Questions: *Author's Point of View Questions Practice*

To answer author's point of view questions, try to get inside the head of the author. What does the author think about the topic? What does the author think about the person about whom he is writing?

Student Directions: As you read the following selection, ask yourself, "What does the author think about Tiffany?" Then answer the question that follows.

Tiffany

When I first met Tiffany, I thought I wanted to be just like her. She moved next door to me the summer before I began fifth grade. She would be in the sixth grade. Tiffany was perfect. She was pretty and smart. It didn't take long before we were fast friends. That summer we played at each other's houses, went to the mall, rode bikes, skateboarded, and just hung out.

The day school began we walked to school together. Tiffany was nervous about not knowing anyone in her class. I told her not to worry. We agreed to meet after school and walk home. When I waved goodbye to Tiffany, I thought she was my best friend.

I waited anxiously for Tiffany after school. She finally came out of school accompanied by two other girls. I waved. Tiffany said something to the two girls and walked over to me. She told me that she would be walking home with her sixth grade classmates, Shelly and Trisha. With a flip of her blonde hair, she walked away. Joining her new friends, she laughed and they brushed by me.

As I slowly walked home, I watched and listened to the trio ahead of me. I was hurt, and I didn't understand. Hadn't we been friends? Was being in the fifth grade really that much of a difference? Maybe she would change her mind, and we would get together later. But I knew that wouldn't happen. I knew I would never trust Tiffany again. I also knew I really *didn't want to be just like Tiffany.*

---

1. What does the author think of Tiffany?

   A. She thinks Tiffany is a good friend.
   B. She thinks Tiffany is an excellent student.
   C. She thinks Tiffany betrayed her friendship.
   D. She thinks Tiffany will change her mind.

Name: _____ Date: _____

Chapter 5: Answering Questions: *Author's Point of View Questions Practice (continued)*

Student Directions: As you read the following selection, ask yourself, "What does the author think about mountain bikes?" Then answer the question that follows.

Mountain Bikes

It is best to shop around before you buy a mountain bike. Mountain bikes need to be built to withstand the harshest of environments. When you first begin to research for the right bike, ask a lot of questions. Start first with bike and sports stores. Ask the sales personnel if they are experienced mountain bikers. What do they prefer? What are the advantages and disadvantages of certain bikes? Take your time.

You can pay anywhere from a few hundred dollars to several thousand dollars for a mountain bike. It is not an inexpensive piece of equipment. Think about the kind of riding you will be doing. Most mountain bike riders don't need to spend thousands of dollars on a good quality bike. The fact is that most mountain bike riding is done on paved roads rather than across rugged terrain.

Find out everything you can so that you can make the best choice in a mountain bike. It is important to make sure you get the right "fit" when choosing a mountain bike. Stand flatfooted astride the bike. There should be 2-4 inches of clearance between you and the top tube on the bike. Most mountain bikes have wheels that are between 17 and 23 inches tall.

Purchasing a mountain bike is an investment. Do your research, and you will discover the adventure of mountain biking, a unique sport that takes you off the beaten path.

---

1. What does the author think of mountain bikes?

    A. It is important to buy the most expensive for quality.
    B. It is important to do the research for the right bike.
    C. Mountain biking can be dangerous.
    D. It is important to join in competitive bike races.

Chapter 6: Test-Taking Skills: *Multiple-Choice Questions*

To answer multiple-choice test questions, use the following guidelines:

1. **Think positive.** Many people worry about taking tests. If you are one of those people, give yourself a "pep talk" before opening the test.

2. **Ask yourself these questions:**

    a. Is it a narrative reading passage?

        If it is a narrative passage, look for the

        **SETTING
        CHARACTERS
        PLOT
        THEME**

    b. Is it an expository reading passage?

        If it is an expository passage, look for the

        **MAIN IDEA
        DETAILS THAT SUPPORT THE MAIN IDEA**

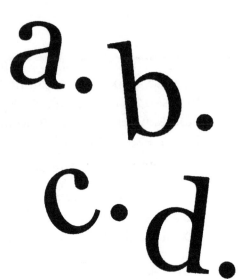

3. **Mark key parts of the text.** As you read, highlight or mark key ideas or make notes in the margin.

    a. Highlight:

        **MAIN IDEAS
        KEY WORDS AND NAMES
        IMPORTANT FACTS, EXAMPLES, ETC.**

4. **Answer the multiple-choice questions.**

    a. If you know the best answer, select which of the choices answers the question.

    b. If you are not sure which is the best answer . . .

        1. Cancel any answers you know are wrong.
        2. Scan the reading for information relating to the question.
        3. Make inferences based on your prior knowledge.

Chapter 6: Test-Taking Skills: *Essay Questions*

To answer essay response questions, follow the following guidelines:

1. **Think positive.** Many people worry about taking tests. If you are one of those people, give yourself a "pep talk" before opening the test.

2. **Read the test question carefully.** What does the question ask you to do?

3. **Think about the "question words."**

   WHAT?
   "What" questions ask you to identify or explain specific things from the reading.

   HOW?
   "How" questions ask how something or someone changes or how different parts are alike or different. "How" questions sometimes ask how something works.

   WHY?
   "Why" questions focus on causes and effects. "Why" questions need specific reasons to be explained. "Why" questions may ask why something is important.

4. **Think about the details from the reading passage.**

5. **Make connections to your own ideas.**

6. **Plan your essay.**

   INTRODUCTION
   Use specific words from the question to state your response to the question.

   BODY
   The body of your essay will give specific details and support for your topic. Use information from the reading passages, but also make a connection to your life or knowledge that you have on the topic.

   CLOSING
   Briefly summarize your main idea or state what you learned from the reading and make a connection to your life.

Name: _____ Date: _____

Chapter 6: Test-Taking Skills: *Test-Taking Practice #1*

Directions: Read the following passage and answer the multiple-choice questions and the extended-response question that follow.

Chief Joseph

Chief Joseph was one of the most famous Native American leaders. He was the great leader of the Nez Perce. He worked his whole life to save and protect his people from war.

The Nez Perce people lived in the same area of America for hundreds of years. Their home was the area where Idaho, Washington, and Oregon meet. These Nez Perce people had great respect for the land and lived by fishing and hunting. When the first white people came to their area in 1805, the Nez Perce people traded goods with them and helped them find their way across the territory.

There were more than 70 bands of Nez Perce people. One band lived in what is now Oregon and was led by Old Joseph. Old Joseph and his wife had a son named Hin mah toe ya laht kit, Thunder Emerging From the Mountains. White men called him Young Joseph.

In 1855, the Nez Perce people and the U.S. government signed a treaty. In the treaty, the Nez Perce agreed to give some of their land to the white settlers. When gold was found on the Nez Perce land, the U.S. government ordered the Nez Perce people to leave their land and live on a reservation. Some of the bands left, but Old Joseph and some other chiefs refused to give up their land.

Old Joseph died, and Young Joseph became Chief Joseph. The new chief believed his people should stay on their land. The U.S. army gave them 30 days to leave. Although many of his people wanted to fight, Chief Joseph knew that too many of his people would die in a war with the white man. Chief Joseph agreed to leave.

Name: _____   Date: _____

Chapter 6: Test-Taking Skills: *Test-Taking Practice #1 (continued)*

Chief Joseph (continued)

As Chief Joseph's people were on their way to the reservation, other bands of Nez Perce joined them. The leaders of these other bands wanted to fight the army. Chief Joseph urged them to go peacefully to the reservation. One night, a few warriors from the other bands attacked some settlers. Three white men were killed. Chief Joseph knew that the army would come after them. The Nez Perce War began. Several battles were fought.

Chief Joseph decided to lead his people into Canada where the army could not follow them. These <u>tenacious</u> people traveled for over three months, never giving in to the terrible conditions. Fewer than 250 Nez Perce warriors fought 13 battles with the U.S. army in that three-month period. More than 80 warriors were killed before they surrendered. Chief Joseph said he would fight no more. When the Nez Perce were stopped by the army, they were only 40 miles away from the Canadian border.

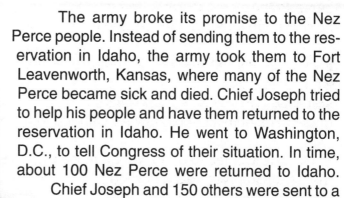

The army broke its promise to the Nez Perce people. Instead of sending them to the reservation in Idaho, the army took them to Fort Leavenworth, Kansas, where many of the Nez Perce became sick and died. Chief Joseph tried to help his people and have them returned to the reservation in Idaho. He went to Washington, D.C., to tell Congress of their situation. In time, about 100 Nez Perce were returned to Idaho. Chief Joseph and 150 others were sent to a reservation in Washington. In 1904 Chief Joseph died. Today, he is remembered as a great leader who was forced into war.

Name: _____ Date: _____

Chapter 6: Test-Taking Skills: *Test-Taking Practice #1— Multiple-Choice Questions*

____ 1. What was the author's main point in writing this passage?

    A.   To describe the wild west

    B.   To show how a courageous leader tried to save his people

    C.   To explain how Indian reservations were managed

    D.   To show how the Nez Perce people lived

____ 2. Where had the Nez Perce people lived for centuries?

    A.   The Kansas and Nebraska area

    B.   In southern California

    C.   The area where Washington, Idaho, and Oregon meet

    D.   The plains of Kansas, Colorado, and Texas

____ 3. Which statement is <u>not</u> true about Chief Joseph?

    A.   He did not want to fight the white man because too many of his people would die.

    B.   He led his people toward Canada to escape the U.S. army.

    C.   He wanted to go to war because the white man had broken the treaty.

    D.   He went to Washington, D.C., to speak for his people.

____ 4. What word best describes the U.S. government?

    A.   Dishonest

    B.   Democratic

    C.   Peaceful

    D.   Honest

Name: _____ Date: _____

Chapter 6: Test-Taking Skills: *Test-Taking Practice #1—Multiple-Choice Questions (continued)*

_____ 5. Why did the U.S. government want to remove the Nez Perce from their homeland?

     A.   It was unsafe because of pollution.

     B.   The Nez Perce were a violent people who often attacked settlers.

     C.   The government wanted to cut the trees in the area for lumber.

     D.   Gold was discovered on Nez Perce land.

_____ 6. Based on what you know about Chief Joseph, what did he want <u>most</u> for his people?

     A.   Their share of the gold found on the land

     B.   To live on the reservation in Idaho

     C.   To stay on their land and fish and hunt

     D.   To live in Washington, D.C.

_____ 7. In the passage, the Nez Perce are described as <u>tenacious</u>. What does tenacious mean?

     A.   Afraid

     B.   Determined

     C.   Warlike

     D.   Weak

     E.   Relaxed

_____ 8. Which best describes the author's point of view? The author thought that Chief Joseph and his people ...

     A.   should have obeyed the order to go to the reservation.

     B.   were guilty of starting the Nez Perce War.

     C.   were betrayed by the American government.

     D.   were foolish to try to escape the U.S. army.

Name: _____   Date: _____

Chapter 6: Test-Taking Skills: *Test-Taking Practice #1— Essay Response Questions*

Directions: Answer the next question on the lines below.

How did Chief Joseph demonstrate that he was a courageous leader who tried to save his people? Use information from the story and your own ideas to specifically support your answer.

_____

_____

_____

_____

_____

_____

_____

_____

_____

_____

_____

_____

_____

_____

_____

_____

_____

Name: _____ Date: _____

Chapter 6: Test-Taking Skills: *Test-Taking Practice #2*

Directions: Read the following selection and answer the multiple-choice questions and the essay response question that follow.

September 1

Lakeland PTA
Middle School
1237 Monroe
Lakeland, WA 99754

Dear parents, teachers, and interested community members:

As a fifth grader at Lakeland Middle School and the Student Council President, I am writing on behalf of the 700 middle-school students at Lakeland Middle School. We are asking for your support in saving our Speech and Drama Club. An administrative decision was made to eliminate the Speech and Drama Club in order to save $1,000 from the school budget.

The majority of the student body here at Lakeland has strong feelings about the Speech and Drama Club. It has been a part of our school for 15 years. More than 100 students are involved in the two performances done each year. Some are involved in acting and presenting; others are involved in costuming and constructing the sets. Even more students are involved in the advertising and marketing. Many of the students continue in speech and drama performances in junior high and senior high. Many students have competed in speech and drama competitions and won awards for their performances. The Speech and Drama Club has been of great benefit to our school.

The students at Lakeland Middle School have begun a letter-writing campaign to the school board, the teachers, and the parents. The response so far has been very positive. We have received over $100 in donations. I have also attached petitions signed by over 80 percent of the student body.

The students at Lakeland Middle School hope that you can help. We also want you to know we will do our part to help support our Speech and Drama Club. We appreciate all your organization does to support our school.

Sincerely,

Timeka Johnson
Lakeland Middle School Student Council President

Name: _____   Date: _____

Chapter 6: Test-Taking Skills: *Test-Taking Practice #2— Multiple-Choice Questions*

_____ 1.   Timeka Johnson's letter contains all of the following except …
   A.   examples.
   B.   threats.
   C.   an offer to help.
   D.   conclusions.

_____ 2.   You can tell from the letter that the Speech and Drama Club is no longer supported by …
   A.   the school's administration.
   B.   the school board.
   C.   the students.
   D.   the community.

_____ 3.   According to the letter, the Speech and Drama Club was eliminated on the basis of …
   A.   complaints from parents.
   B.   lack of quality.
   C.   its cost.
   D.   failure to involve students.

_____ 4.   The letter was written to convince the …
   A.   student council.
   B.   school administration.
   C.   school board.
   D.   PTA.

_____ 5.   The tone of the letter is …
   A.   respectful.
   B.   demanding.
   C.   apologetic.
   D.   funny.

_____ 6.   We can see that Timeka Johnson thinks that the student council president should represent …
   A.   the school board.
   B.   the student body.
   C.   the PTA.
   D.   the parents.

Name: _____ Date: _____

Chapter 6: Test-Taking Skills: *Test-Taking Practice #2—Essay Response Questions*

Directions: Answer the next question on the lines below.

How does Timeka Johnson demonstrate that the student body supports the Speech and Drama Club? Use information from the story and your own ideas to specifically support your answer.

_____

_____

_____

_____

_____

_____

_____

_____

_____

_____

_____

_____

_____

_____

Appendices: *Table of Contents*

Name: _____ Date: _____

Reading Survey

Directions: Answer the following questions about your reading habits.

1. How many books do you have of your own? _____

2. How many books have you read this month? _____

3. What kinds of books do you like to read? _____

   _____

4. Who is your favorite author? _____

5. What magazines or newspapers do you like to read? _____

   _____

6. How did you learn to read? _____

   _____

7. When you are reading and come to something you don't know, what do you do?

   _____

   _____

8. What makes a good reader? _____

   _____

   _____

9. Do you think you are a good reader? Why or why not? _____

   _____

10. Why do you think reading well is important? _____

   _____

   _____

Name: _____   Date: _____

Reading Attitude Survey

Directions: Circle the answer that is most true about you.

A = Often   B = A few times a month   C = Sometimes   D = Never/Almost never

How often do you do the following?

1.	Talk to my family or friends about a good book I have read.	A B C D
2.	Reread a favorite book.	A B C D
3.	Read at home books that are not part of schoolwork.	A B C D
4.	Read books by the same author.	A B C D
5.	Go to the library to check out a book.	A B C D

How often is each of the following true for you and your reading?

A = Often   B = A few times a month   C = Sometimes   D = Never/Almost never

6.	I can understand what I am assigned to read in school.	A B C D
7.	I feel proud about how I read.	A B C D
8.	I know reading helps me learn about many subjects.	A B C D
9.	I enjoy reading aloud in class.	A B C D
10.	I like to listen to a book being read aloud.	A B C D
11.	I like to read.	A B C D

Name: _____   Date: _____

Teacher/Student Interview Questions

About book selection

1. Why do you select a book to read? _____

   _____

2. How do you know the book is one you can read? _____

   _____

Before reading

3. What do you do before you begin to read a story/novel? _____

   _____

4. What do you do before you read a magazine or newspaper article? _____

   _____

5. What do you do before reading a science or social studies textbook? _____

   _____

During reading

6. If you are reading alone and can't figure out a word, what do you do? _____

   _____

7. If you are reading alone and don't know the meaning of a word, what do you do? _____

   _____

8. What do you do if you don't understand paragraphs or whole pages? _____

   _____

After reading

9. What do you think about when you finish your reading? _____

   _____

What else do you want me to know about your reading?

   _____

   _____

   _____

Name: _____ Date: _____

Student Self-Assessment of Reading

Directions: Check the box that indicates your level of understanding while reading.

I Can …	I Try	Sometimes	Always
Remember things I already know.			
Make predictions about what will come next.			
Summarize what I read.			
Sound out words I don't know.			
Give people detailed facts about what I have read.			
Make pictures in my mind as I read.			
Figure out what the author means from different parts of my reading.			
Try reading words I don't know.			
Use expression when I read aloud.			
Guess the meaning of a word because it looks like another word I know.			
Break words into syllables.			
Ask questions to myself or to the author as I read.			

Strategies Good Readers Use
(Before/During/After Reading)

Keep these strategies handy for reference while you are reading.

- Selects a book appropriate for his or her reading level

- Uses skimming and scanning to review a text

- Uses prior knowledge

- Makes predictions

- Asks questions

- Pauses to reflect, to summarize, to highlight, or to take notes

- Uses context clues

- Rereads

- Uses word analysis to figure out unknown words

- Identifies main ideas

- Makes inferences

- Draws conclusions

- Notes cause and effect

- Knows when they do not understand and self-monitors reading

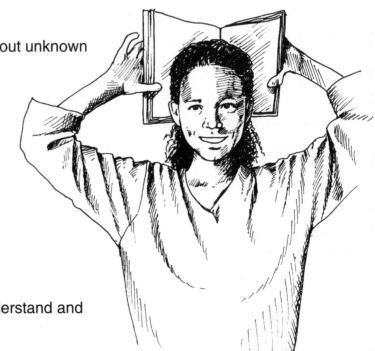

Name: _____ Date: _____

What I Read

Directions: Record what you read for your reader's notebook.

What I Read for Myself	What I Read for My Teacher/School

Name: _____ Date: _____

What I Write

Directions: Record what you write for your writer's notebook.

What I Write for Myself and to Others	What I Write for My Teacher/School

Name: _____ Date: _____

Peer Talk: The Interview #1

Directions: After you have read a selection, conduct an interview about your reading.

Knowledge:

1. Who are the main characters?

_____

_____

_____

_____

_____

2. What do you know about the author?

_____

_____

_____

_____

3. What happened in the chapter you read?

_____

_____

_____

_____

_____

Name: _____ Date: _____

Peer Talk: The Interview #2

Directions: After you have read a selection, conduct an interview about your reading.

Comprehension:

1. What are two words to describe the main character?

   _____

   _____

2. What do you know about the character's personality?

   _____

   _____

   _____

   _____

   _____

3. Retell the story.

   _____

   _____

   _____

   _____

   _____

   _____

   _____

   _____

Name: _____ Date: _____

Peer Talk: The Interview #3

Directions: After you have read a selection, conduct an interview about your reading.

Application:

1. Create a time line to show what has happened so far in your reading.

2. If you were to write a letter to one of the characters, what would you say?

_____

_____

_____

_____

_____

_____

_____

_____

_____

_____

3. Draw a picture on your own paper illustrating the most important scene in your reading.

Name: _____   Date: _____

Peer Talk: The Interview #4

Directions: After you have read a selection, conduct an interview about your reading.

Analysis:

1. How would you solve the problem in the story differently if you could?

   _____

   _____

   _____

   _____

   _____

   _____

2. What do you think is the author's message or main theme?

   _____

   _____

   _____

   _____

3. What other books have you read that have a similar message or theme? How are they different/alike?

   _____

   _____

   _____

   _____

Name: _____ Date: _____

Peer Talk: The Interview #5

Directions: After you have read a selection, conduct an interview about your reading.

Synthesis:

1. What do you predict will happen next?

_____

_____

_____

_____

2. If a sequel were written to this book, what would happen?

_____

_____

_____

_____

3. If this book were given an award, what would it receive and why?

_____

_____

_____

_____

Name: _____ Date: _____

Peer Talk: The Interview #6

Directions: After you have read a selection, conduct an interview about your reading.

Evaluation:

1. Would you recommend the book for other students to read? Why or why not?

_____

_____

_____

_____

2. Did the characters make the right decisions? Would you have done the same? Why?

_____

_____

_____

_____

3. Is the theme of the book realistic for students today? Why or why not?

_____

_____

_____

_____

Name: _____   Date: _____

Peer Talk: The Interview #7

Directions: After you have read a selection, conduct an interview about your reading.

Making Connections:

1. What in the book reminds you of something that happened to you or someone you know?

   _____

   _____

   _____

   _____

2. Did this book remind you of any other book you have read? How were the two books similar?

   _____

   _____

   _____

   _____

3. What was something you learned about life, people, or yourself as you read this book?

   _____

   _____

   _____

   _____

Name: _____ Date: _____

Using Predictions to Make Connections

Predicting

Student Directions: As you read, pay close attention to the parts of the text when you find yourself making a prediction. Using the form below, jot down the first and last word of the passage or identify the picture that helped you make a prediction. Then write down your prediction. When you have finished your reading, go back and check to see if your predictions actually happened. Then write down what really happened.

Passage or Picture: _____

Prediction: _____

_____

Was your prediction right? _____ If not, what did happen? _____

_____

Passage or Picture: _____

Prediction: _____

_____

Was your prediction right? _____ If not, what did happen? _____

_____

Passage or Picture: _____

Prediction: _____

_____

Was your prediction right? _____ If not, what did happen? _____

_____

Name: _____   Date: _____

Using Predictions to Make Connections

Making Connections to Your Own Life

Student Directions: As you read, pay close attention to the parts of the text when you find yourself making **a connection to your own life**. Using the form below, jot down the first and last word of the passage or identify the picture where you made the connection to your life. Then write down your connection.

Passage or Picture: _____

_____

Connection to My Life: _____

_____

_____

_____

_____

Passage or Picture: _____

_____

Connection to My Life: _____

_____

_____

_____

Name: _____ Date: _____

Using Predictions to Make Connections

Making Connections to Another Text You Have Read

Student Directions: As you read, pay close attention to the parts of the text where you find yourself making **a connection to another text that you have read**. Using the form below, jot down the first and last word of the passage or identify the picture where you made the connection to another text. Then write down your connection.

Passage or Picture: _____

_____

Connection to Another Text I've Read: _____

_____

_____

_____

_____

Passage or Picture: _____

_____

Connection to Another Text I've Read: _____

_____

_____

_____

Name: _____ Date: _____

Using Predictions to Make Connections

Making Connections to the World

Student Directions: As you read, pay close attention to the parts of the text where you find yourself making **a connection to other knowledge you have about the world.** Using the form below, jot down the first and last word of the passage or identify the picture where you made the connection to other knowledge. Then write down your connection.

Passage or Picture: _____

_____

Connection to the World: _____

_____

_____

_____

_____

Passage or Picture: _____

_____

Connection to the World: _____

_____

_____

_____

_____

Name: _____ Date: _____

Questioning

Student Directions: As you read, stop and think about the questions you have. Good readers ask questions **BEFORE** they read, **DURING** their reading, and **AFTER** they read. Highlight or tab with a sticky note where you have questions, then record those questions in the following boxes. Also record any answers to your questions that you discover. You can do this during your reading or after you have finished reading.

Questions I Have Before I Read

1. _____

2. _____

3. _____

Any Answers? _____

_____

Questions I Have During My Reading

1. _____

2. _____

3. _____

Any Answers? _____

_____

Questions I Have After I Read

1. _____

2. _____

3. _____

Any Answers? _____

_____

Name: _____   Date: _____

Reading Comprehension Graphic Organizer

Directions: As you read a selection, use the graphic organizers to keep track of the most important information.

I. BEFORE YOU READ

Read the title of the article and the first paragraph.

Stop/Think/Predict

1. What do you think this article will explain?

   _____

   _____

   _____

2. Preview the article by looking at any photographs or illustrations.

3. What information does the picture clarify for you? Record your ideas.

The picture of	tells me…

Name: _____ Date: _____

Reading Comprehension Graphic Organizer

II. WHILE YOU READ

1. Use the graphic organizer to keep track of the details of your reading selection.

2. Record information that seems important and any questions that you have as you read.

Identify Main Idea
Information/Question:
Information/Question:
Information/Question:
Information/Question:

Name: _____ Date: _____

Narrative Reading Sequence Map

To keep track of the plot it can be useful to keep a sequence map as you read.

Directions: As you read a narrative story, keep track of the story elements by asking yourself and the author questions.

Sequence Map

```
┌─────────────────────────────────────────────┐
│                                             │
└─────────────────────────────────────────────┘
                     ▼
┌─────────────────────────────────────────────┐
│                                             │
└─────────────────────────────────────────────┘
                     ▼
┌─────────────────────────────────────────────┐
│                                             │
└─────────────────────────────────────────────┘
                     ▼
┌─────────────────────────────────────────────┐
│                                             │
└─────────────────────────────────────────────┘
                     ▼
┌─────────────────────────────────────────────┐
│                                             │
└─────────────────────────────────────────────┘
                     ▼
┌─────────────────────────────────────────────┐
│                                             │
└─────────────────────────────────────────────┘
```

Name: _____ Date: _____

Narrative Reading Story Map

Directions: Check your comprehension. Fill in the following graphic organizer.

Title: _____

Setting:

    * When _____

    * Where _____

Characters:

    * _____

    * _____

    * _____

Plot: (What are the events in order?)

    * _____

    * _____

    * _____

    * _____

    * _____

    * _____

Theme: _____

_____

_____

_____

Name: _____ Date: _____

Expository Reading: Supporting Details

Directions: Fill in the following information about your reading.

Paragraph # _____

Topic Sentence _____

_____

Important Supporting Details

    1. _____

    2. _____

    3. _____

    4. _____

Paragraph # _____

Topic Sentence _____

_____

Important Supporting Details

    1. _____

    2. _____

    3. _____

    4. _____

Answer Keys

P. 42–48 Chapter 3: Graphic Organizer Practice 1

Answers may vary slightly. Possible answers are given.

I. 1. It is the time in Egypt's history when Hatshepsut was pharoah.
    3. Answers will vary.
II. 2. Answers will vary.
III. Main Idea: Queen Hatshepsut of Egypt was one of the greatest women rulers of all time.

Supporting Details:
1. Hatshepsut's husband died, and her son was only an infant.
2. She was the only adult in the royal family who could rule.
3. Hatshepsut had new temples built.
4. She sent trading expeditions to distant lands.
5. She was respected by her father's supporters.
6. She went into battle herself.
7. Hatshepsut's daughter died, and her son took over as king before Hatshepsut died.
8. Thutmose III tried to destroy all the evidence that Hatshepsut had been queen.

Closing: Egypt's Queen Hatshepsut remains one of the most important women in history. Her strong leadership allowed Egypt to prosper for many years.

P. 49–56 Chapter 3: Graphic Organizer Practice 2

Answers may vary slightly. Possible answers are given.

I. 1. It will explain how the calendar came to be.
    3. Answers will vary.
II. Answers will vary.

III. Problem:
Who: The Egyptians, the Romans, Julius Caesar, Pope Gregory XIII
What: They tried to develop an accurate calandar.
Why: To correctly predict the changing seasons for planting and harvesting
Solution:
Attempted Solutions:
1. Egyptian astronomers created a 365-day calendar with 12 months divided into 30 days each. There were five extra days at the end of the year.
2. Julius Caesar had Sosigenes develop a solar calendar with 365 days. Half the months had 30 days, half had 31, and February had one less day. A leap day was added to February every four years.
3. Pope Gregory XIII eliminated a few leap years and took ten days out of 1582.
Results:
1. The Egyptian year was shorter than the solar year by one-fourth day. After many years, the calendar was no longer correct with the seasons.
2. The Julian calendar worked well for a while, but it was 11 minutes longer than a solar year. By the late 1500s, the Julian calendar was 10 days too long.
3. The Gregorian calendar almost exactly matches the solar year.
End Result: With the Gregorian calendar, we do not lose or gain days compared to the solar year.
Closing: Our calendar was developed over thousands of years. After attempts by the Egyptians and Romans, we finally have a calendar that doesn't lose days.

P. 58   Chapter 4: Narrative Reading Practice—Sequence Map

Answers may vary slightly. Possible answers are given.

- Megan's dad went into business for himself and moved the family from Oklahoma to Missouri.
- Megan had to leave her best friend, Sara.
- Megan thought school was boring, she didn't like the teacher, and she had no friends.
- Megan got to the bus late one day, and a girl offered her a seat.
- The girl offered to show Megan a baby calf at her house.
- This girl's name was also Sara.

P. 61   Chapter 4: Narrative Reading Practice—Story Map

Title: It Couldn't Be!

Setting: When: Present-day
            Where: near Fulton, Missouri—
            mostly on the school bus

Characters: Megan, her dad, her mom, Miss Ramus, Sara Peterson

Plot: Same as outlined in Sequence Map activity above.

Theme: Sometimes there are strange coincidences in life.

P. 64   Chapter 4: Expository Reading Practice

First Paragraph

Topic Sentence: These are the animals and trees that today make up the Petrified Forest National Park.

1. … you will see rainbow-colored stone columns and logs where living trees once stood.
2. These are fossils of ancient reptiles and amphibians that roamed the world centuries ago, …
3. … it was a lush green land with streams where strange amphibians and reptiles lived.
4. The land was covered in thick forests of giant trees.

Second Paragraph

Topic Sentence: How could living things be turned to stone?

1. Trees died, were washed away by flood water into marshes, sank to the bottom, and were covered by sediment.
2. Volcanoes erupted, and ash spewed into the marshes.
3. The ash dissolved, soaked through to the trees, and replaced the decaying wood with silica.
4. When the marshes dried, the silica hardened into quartz.

P. 66   Third Paragraph

Topic Sentence: The hills were worn away, and thousands of petrified logs and fossils were unearthed.

1. More than 60 million years ago, pressure from the earth's inner core caused the land to bulge and form hills of sandstone, mud, and clay.
2. These hills contained the petrified trees and animals from millions of years before.
3. Over the years, rain, snow, and ice eroded away the soft stone.

Fourth Paragraph

Topic Sentence: Two thousand years later, the first people to wander into this breathtaking landscape were the Anasazi, a tribe of prehistoric American Indians.

1. They are called the "Ancient Ones" by the Navajo Indians who live there today.
2. The Anasazi farmed the land and built houses that were joined together to make a pueblo (village).
3. Puerco Ruins is part of the Petrified Forest. It was built 900 years ago with 75 rooms, and it contains petroglyphs.
4. The Anasazi left the Petrified Forest in search of land with more water.

P. 69   Chapter 5: Main Idea Questions
Explanations may vary.
1. D, It talks about why people would want to be rock climbers, not the equipment, the dangers, or the procedure.
2. C, Rock climbers are mainly concerned with not falling down, and that is what the title illustrates.

P. 71–72   Chapter 5: Detail Questions Practice
1. free climbing
2. Rock climbing is movement over rock. Mountaineering is movement over rock, snow, ice, and glaciers. Different mountaineering skills would not be needed by a rock climber.
3. Bouldering is simple rock climbing on a large boulder. You try to cross the rock from left to right (or vice versa) without a rope.
4. You need a boulder big enough to climb, comfortable clothes, and walking shoes or hiking boots.
5. You should plan to go with a partner and learn about first aid.

P. 74   Chapter 5: Vocabulary Questions Practice
1. C
2. B

P. 76–77   Chapter 5: Sequence Questions Practice
1. A
2. B

P. 80   Chapter 5: Inference Questions Practice
Answers may vary. Possible answers are given.
1. Children may have had health problems later on because of the dust and hunger they suffered.
- Children had to sleep with wet towels over their faces to help filter out the dust and sand. Carloads of homeless and hungry men, women, and children …

2. Farmers were surrounded by the eroding land, and their whole income came from farming the land.
- For four years, savage dust storms destroyed the farmland, crops, and people's lives. Eventually hundreds of thousands of people were forced to leave their homes and their lands.

P. 82   Chapter 5: Theme Questions Practice
1. People may have hidden talents that we never suspect.
2. Josh was very quiet and nerdy, but when he got on stage, he was really funny. He was still quiet and shy after the talent show, but at least the rest of the kids gave him a chance to be involved.

P. 84   Chapter 5: Author's Point of View Questions Practice
1. C

P. 85   Chapter 5: Author's Point of View Questions Practice
1. B

P. 90–91   Chapter 6: Test-Taking Practice #1—Multiple-Choice Questions
1. B
2. C
3. C
4. A
5. D
6. C
7. B
8. C

P. 92   Chapter 6: Test-Taking Practice #1—Essay Response Questions
Answers will vary.

P. 94   Chapter 6: Test-Taking Practice #2—Multiple-Choice Questions
1. B
2. A
3. C
4. D
5. A
6. B

P. 95   Chapter 6: Test-Taking Practice #1—Essay Response Questions
Answers will vary.

Bibliography

Allen, Janet. 1995. *It's Never Too Late: Leading Adolescents to Lifelong Literacy.* Portsmouth, NH: Heinemann.

Allen, Janet and Kyle Gonzales. 1998. *There's Room for Me Here: Literacy Workshop in the Middle Schools.* York, ME; Stenhouse.

Allington, Richard. 1997. In *Building a Knowledge Base in Readings,* eds. Jane Braunger and Jan Lewis. Newark, DE: International Reading Association.

Atwell, Nancie. 1998. *In the Middle: New Understandings About Writing, Reading, and Learning.* Portsmouth, NH: Heinemann.

Burke, Jim. 1999. *I Hear America Reading: Why We Read - What We Read.* Portsmouth, NH: Heinemann.

Burke, Jim. 1999. *The English Teacher's Companion: A Complete Guide to Classroom, Curriculum, and the Profession.* Portsmouth, NH: Heinemann.

Calkins, Lucy. 1986. *The Art of Teaching Writing.* Portsmouth, NH: Heinemann.

Culhan, Ruth. 1998. *Picture Books: An Annotated Bibliography.* Portland, OR: Northwest Regional Educational Laboratory.

Cunningham, Patricia and Richard Allington. 1999. *Classrooms That Work: They Can All Read and Write.* NY: Longman.

Daniels, Harvey. 1994. *Literature Circles: Voice and Choice in the Classroom.* York, ME: Stenhouse.

Fletcher, Ralph and Jean Portalupi. 1998. *Craft Lessons: Teaching Writing K–8.* York, ME: Stenhouse.

Fountas, Irene and Gay Sue Pinnell. 1996. *Guided Reading: Good First Teaching for All Children.* Portsmouth, NH: Heinemann.

Harvey, Stephanie. 1998. *Nonfiction Matters: Reading, Writing and Research in Grades 3–8.* York, ME: Stenhouse.

Johnson, Janet. 1998. *Content Area Reading.* NY: Delmar.

Keene, Ellin and Susan Zimmerman. 1997. *Mosaic of Thought: Teaching Comprehension in a Reader's Workshop.* Portsmouth, NH: Heinemann.

Lane, Barry. 1993. *After the End: Teaching and Learning Creative Revision.* Portsmouth, NH: Heinemann.

Opitz, M. and T. Rasinski. 1999. *Good-Bye Round Robin.* Portsmouth, NH: Heinemann.

Pearson, P.D. and B. Taylor. 1999. *Schools That Beat the Odds.*

Pearson, P.D. and L. Fielding. 1991. "Comprehension Instruction." ed. R. Barr, M. Kamil, P. Mosenthan, and P.D. Pearson. *Handbook of Reading Research,* Vol. 2, pp 815–860. NY: Longman.

Robinson, Linda. 1998. "Understanding Middle School Students." In *Into Focus: Understanding and Creating Middle School Readers,* ed. Kylene Beers and Barbara G. Samuels. Norwood, MA: Christopher-Gordon.

Routman, Regie. 2000. *Conversations: Strategies for Teaching, Learning, and Evaluating.* Portsmouth, NH: Heinemann.

Weaver, Constance. 1998. *Practicing What We Know: Informed Reading Instruction.* Urbana, IL: National Council of Teachers of English.

Weaver, Constance. 1998. *Reconsidering a Balanced Approach to Reading.* Urbana, IL: National Council of Teachers of English.